Singing School

Also by Jon Stallworthy

POETRY

The Astronomy of Love
Out of Bounds
Root and Branch
Positives
Hand in Hand
The Apple Barrel
A Familiar Tree
The Anzac Sonata: New and Selected Poems
The Guest from the Future
Rounding the Horn: Collected Poems

ANTHOLOGIES

The Penguin Book of Love Poetry
The Oxford Book of War Poetry
First Lines: Poems Written in Youth, from Herbert to Heaney

EDITED

Wilfred Owen: The Complete Poems and Fragments
The Poems of Wilfred Owen
Henry Reed: Collected Poems

BIOGRAPHY

Wilfred Owen
Louis MacNeice

LITERARY CRITICISM

Between the Lines: W.B. Yeats's Poetry in the Making
Vision and Revision in Yeats's Last Poems

TRANSLATIONS
(WITH PETER FRANCE)

Alexander Blok: Selected Poems
Boris Pasternak: Selected Poems

Singing School

The Making of a Poet

JON STALLWORTHY

JOHN MURRAY
Albemarle Street, London

First published in 1998
by John Murray (Publishers) Ltd,
50 Albemarle Street, London W1X 4BD

A catalogue record for this book is available from the British Library

ISBN 0-7195-5715 1

Typeset in 11.5 pt Bembo by Servis Filmsetting Ltd, Manchester

Printed and bound in Great Britain by
The University Press, Cambridge

An aged man is but a paltry thing,
A tattered coat upon a stick, unless
Soul clap its hands and sing, and louder sing
For every tatter in its mortal dress,
Nor is there singing school but studying
Monuments of its own magnificence;
And therefore I have sailed the seas and come
To the holy city of Byzantium.

W.B. Yeats, 'Sailing to Byzantium'

Poetic schools existed in Ireland before Christianity, and the training poets received in them had its origins in the druidic learning associated with the religion of Celtic Gaul, Britain and Ireland. . . .

Scholars were in residence at the schools from October to Easter. Teaching was conducted orally, but there was also instruction from Irish and Latin manuscripts; the course of study often lasted seven years; and tuition was given in language, grammatical learning, metrics, genealogy, law, Latin, dinnshen-chas [place-name lore], mythology, and history. Students composed alone in the dark on allotted subjects and in given metres, reciting their verses in public performance.

Robert Welch, ed., *The Oxford Companion to Irish Literature*

Contents

Illustrations

Illustrations

The author and the publisher would like to thank the following for permission to reproduce illustrations: pp. 26, 48 and 51, Dragon School, Oxford; p. 34, Claire Blunden; p. 49, Richard Sorabji; pp. 54 and 66, Barbara Lynam; p. 71, Geoffrey Creighton Studios; p. 77, Ros Pattern; p. 84, from Gwen Raverat, *Period Piece*, Faber and Faber Ltd; pp. 86 and 88, Richard Keynes; p. 202, Peter Placito; p. 215, Herbert Felton, FRPS; and p. 223, A. P. Watt Ltd.

Genealogy

IT WAS A small flat, sparsely furnished: I remember only the red map and the white rug. Neither belonged to us.

If my parents had chosen the map – or at least if my father had chosen it – it would have been a map of the world, the predominantly pink map of their New Zealand childhoods. My mother might perhaps have chosen the blood-red map of the imaginary island that hung above my bed, because she valued imagination. I couldn't read the names of the forests and mountain ranges that loomed above me as I slept, but seem to remember talk of buried treasure and dragons. Certainly, dragons were in the air one afternoon when, lying on the white rug with a pencil in my hand, I laboriously copied words from a white card into a lined exercise book. There were two words. I had probably written the shorter one before. The longer one was a pain. I wanted to play outside, but I wanted to go to school even more, and you couldn't go to the Dragon School unless you could read and write. Everyone at the Wayside Nursery wanted to go to the Dragon School, particularly those with brothers and sisters there. They had a sandpit at the Dragon School.

First, however, I had to learn to put the letters of the longer word in the right order (without the card, which my mother had removed from the rug). She said it was *our* name – my father's, hers, and mine. I didn't understand that: my father's name was

John (the same as mine except that it had an *h* in the middle) and hers was Peggy. It hadn't always been Peggy, she said, and it hadn't always been Stallworthy.

★

Her story, which by slow accretion like a coral reef would become my story, began in Scotland with the birth of John Howie. Forty years later, by then the manager of a Liverpool bank and a chronic asthmatic, he was advised that only a long sea-voyage could restore his health. He closed his ledgers, handed over his keys, and in 1887 sailed for New Zealand. Did he intend to return? His daughter never knew. Her story said only that, a year after landing, he married Maggie Todd, a lively young woman half his age, and set up house with her near Waikiwi on the southern tip of South Island. He gave his house a braw Scottish name, 'Glenorchy', and together they raised vegetables and children: Helen Merrie, Elizabeth Wright, William Gladstone, Mary Findlay, John Ruskin, James Jeffries, Arthur Hallam, Alfred Tennyson, Allan Ramsay, and Margaret Wright. The names of John Howie's sons (Maggie named her daughters) reveal – as his diaries reveal – his principal interest: the lives and works of Eminent Victorians. Reading became his occupation. Sitting in his big chair, turning the pages, he would pause only to copy a favourite passage in his elegant copperplate hand into a commonplace book, until, in 1915, life interrupted his contemplation of literature.

The Empire was at war: 'at home' and 'down under', men were queuing outside recruiting offices, and William Gladstone Howie, a volunteer in the Australian and New Zealand Army Corps (ANZAC), received his embarkation orders for an unheard-of – perhaps because unpink – point on the map, the Dardanelles. One morning, his 7-year-old sister Margaret (already known as Peggy) woke to find on her pillow a calico doll she had long coveted across the counter of the local Stores;

The Howies of 'Glenorchy': William Gladstone is in the middle of
the back row, Peggy in the middle of the front row

down the corridor, Ramsay found on *his* pillow a small violin –
presents bought with Bill's embarkation allowance. Later that
morning, their eldest sister, a teacher at the Waikiwi School,
stood with Peggy and Ramsay in the playground to watch Bill's
detachment of the Otago Mounted Rifles riding off to war.
They never saw him again. He was wounded at Gallipoli and
died at Gibraltar. His heartbroken father died soon after.

Maggie, younger and more resilient, held the rest of the
family together and, when Hallam and Tennyson won places at
Otago University, she moved to Dunedin to be near them.
Tennyson soon became friends with a fellow medical student
from the northern promontory of North Island. John
Stallworthy had been born in Dargaville, where his father – a
father then (though not later) as hard as Tennyson's had been
soft – owned and managed a local newspaper. Work was what

The Stallworthys of Dargaville: John is at the right of the picture

mattered in the Stallworthy household. Pleasure had no place at all. Money for a boy's rugby boots was out of the question, even for a boy who delivered his father's newspapers on horseback before dawn and after dusk each day. John, however, found a pound note blowing in the street, bought his own boots, and played his way into school and university rugby XVs. He was also captain of the university tennis team, toured Australia with the debating team, was editor of the university *Review*, and President of its Students' Association. Even so, he was almost expelled for his part in a campaign to unseat an unpopular Master of his college. The Master's chimney was stuffed with wet sacks and every undertaker in Dunedin, notified (prematurely) of his death, was asked to call – each at a different hour – to collect the body.

The President of the Students' Association had other risky pastimes. He and his friends converted some derelict tennis courts into a dirt-track for their motorbikes, but to their surprise (and perhaps his own) he was persuaded to give this up by Tennyson Howie's youngest sister. A gipsy fortune-teller at a fair had told her things about her family she thought no outsider could have known. As for her Fortune, that was said to be threatened by a Death: 'Someone important to you is doing something dangerous and must be stopped.' Peggy Howie must by then have been important to John Stallworthy because he stopped.

He graduated from Otago with distinction, a gold medal in surgery, gynaecology and obstetrics, and a travelling scholarship to Australia. Naturally left-handed, he had by then taught himself to operate right-handed (able to use the standard instruments and assist right-handed surgeons), but his control of his left hand was to prove an incalculable surgical advantage. On his return from Australia, now qualified as a doctor, he went back to Dunedin and called on Mrs Howie. When she showed him into the front room and her husband's chair – the chair reserved since his death for the senior son present – he took it as a good omen for the success of his mission, and he left the house her prospective son-in-law.

He had been appointed to an Auckland hospital and was on casualty duty one evening when a little girl in a deep coma was carried in. Her widowed mother, Nancy Jones, could only say she had found her daughter unconscious and been unable to revive her. JS (as he would always be known in hospitals) worked on her all night: at dawn her pulse was stronger and at midday she regained consciousness. She was kept in under observation for some days and tests were undertaken that failed to yield any positive results. Then suddenly, on her birthday, she collapsed again. JS was off duty, but hearing the news he hurried to her bedside and once again his treatment was successful. As he was about to leave the ward, he noticed among the birthday presents on her bedside table a bag of sweets and, on an impulse, pocketed a couple which he sent off for analysis. The lab report showed a high arsenic content. The police were informed and the girl's mother charged with attempted murder.

The case was widely reported in the papers and, when it came to court, the defence counsel, a prominent criminal lawyer called Templeton, set out to destroy the credibility of the principal prosecution witness, a young doctor whose debating experience came to his aid in the course of fierce cross-questioning.

'Doctor Stallworthy,' Templeton began, 'it *is* Doctor Stallworthy, isn't it?'

'Yes.'

'How long have you been qualified?'

'Three months.'

'Only three months? Then you haven't seen many patients in the condition in which Miss Jones was admitted?'

'No.'

Templeton made much of the witness's inexperience, and their exchanges became heated until abruptly and dramatically terminated. The barrister had a pile of books beside him. He lifted one and said:

'Doctor Stallworthy, you're no doubt familiar with *X*' (and he named a famous textbook).

'Yes.' Templeton put the book down and took up another.

'And you're no doubt familiar with *Y*.'

'Yes.' Templeton put that book down and took up a third.

'And you're no doubt familiar with *Z*.'

'No.'

'You're *not* familiar with *Z*? I find it surprising that a doctor – even a newly qualified doctor – should not be familiar with a book to be found and referred to in every hospital in the country. But since you're not familiar with it, let me read you something that will interest you.' He named a disease – not known to the witness – and read out a list of symptoms resembling those of Miss Jones.

'What do you say to that?' he asked.

'I say can I see the book?'

'Come, come, young man, don't prevaricate!'

'Can I see the book?'

'You're wasting the court's time! Answer my question.'

'Can I see the book?'

'Show him the book,' said the judge.

Templeton slammed it down on the table and stormed out of court. The book was passed to the witness who, checking the disease, discovered that Templeton had omitted a range of symptoms not displayed by Miss Jones. He lost the case and his client was convicted of attempted murder.

Barrister and witness met once more, on the steps of the courthouse, after the trial had ended. The doctor was embarrassed, but not so the barrister who could not have been more genial and said: 'They tell me you've just won a travelling scholarship to England.'

'Yes.'

'My congratulations. You're a clever young man and I should like to help you. My brother is a Lecturer at London University. Let me give you his address.' And he wrote it on a card that his astonished adversary knew he would never use.

John Stallworthy and Peggy Howie were married in January 1934, and some months later – by which time Peggy was pregnant – set off for England in a rusty freighter called the *Port Sydney*. Her crew said she should have been refitted in New Zealand, but the owners insisted the refit be undertaken (more cheaply) on the Clyde, a decision that almost cost them the ship. Her rudder chains snapped in mountainous seas as she rounded the Horn in mid-winter. While the crew – including JS, the ship's doctor – struggled to repair the damage, Peggy was strapped into her bunk but, even so, bruised the whole length of her body. She didn't however miscarry, as her husband feared she might, and their child rounded the cape in calmer waters.

The voyage did have its lighter moments, as when the ship's lugubrious steward entered the doctor's cabin without knocking and, finding his wife naked, said: 'The lady's bath's ready, sir', and withdrew.

Landing in England, they rented a small flat from a landlady, called Jemima, who proceeded to steal their only clock and many of their wedding presents. By the time the police found the pawn tickets under her carpet, she had transferred her assets into her sister's name and was technically bankrupt. This blow coincided with another. JS had a junior appointment at Bart's Hospital, but had been too shy to ask the salary. When, at the end of his first month's work, no cheque arrived, he made an embarrassed enquiry and was told he should count himself fortunate to have the job and could not expect a salary *as well*. He soon learnt that most of the other junior doctors had private incomes, or at least an allowance from a father 'in the profession', and many had ambiguous (or, worse, unambiguous) feelings about colonials with ill-fitting suits and discordant vowels. JS himself had ambiguous feelings about one of the most patrician lords of the wards: Geoffrey Keynes (Rugby and Cambridge), brother of Maynard Keynes, friend of Rupert Brooke, husband of Charles Darwin's granddaughter, a successful surgeon with a reputation also as a bibliographer, book-collector, and literary man about London. Had he and his antipodean 'dresser' been granted foreknowledge in 1934 that they would become friends, it is hard to know which would have been the more astonished.

If the rewards of working for no salary, in wards where the cut of a suit seemed sometimes as important as that of a scalpel, were not immediately apparent to her husband, Peggy knew from the first that England was the promised land. It was 'home', home to her father's heroes: Gladstone, Hallam and Tennyson had walked its streets. John Keats had been an impecunious 'dresser' here before *her* John. What little she knew of English history and literature was enough to endow the autumnal monochrome of suburban London with the colours of Romance.

Money was the problem – and even more of a problem when, after the unmasking of Jemima, they moved to a more attractive (and expensive) flat in Mortlake Road, close to Kew Gardens. There they learnt the falsity of one proverb and the truth of another: two cannot live as cheaply as one, but they took good care of the pennies and the pounds took care of themselves. Every evening, while John bent over the textbooks he had to master for the exams he had still to pass, Peggy entered the day's expenses in her account-book. On Saturdays and special occasions, they would treat themselves to baked beans on toast (costing ninepence a portion) at a Lyons Corner House in central London.

I like to think my birth, in January 1935, might have justified (at least) such a celebration. Another event, shortly after, certainly did: my father's appointment as a Resident Surgical Officer at the Chelsea Hospital for Women. He was to have a salary there and, more importantly, was apprenticed to a great pelvic surgeon called Victor Bonney, whose series of five hundred Wertheim hysterectomies would earn him a place in medical history. My father thought Bonney's hands the most beautiful in the world (with the exception of his Peggy's), gentle but not soft, as they made their swift incisions and decisions. When, two years later, he left the Chelsea Hospital, he asked Bonney for a photograph of his hands. For the rest of his life this hung in his consulting rooms, facing his desk, where had he been a priest one might have expected a crucifix, palms outstretched and pierced with nails. My father revered those hands and measured his own handiwork by the memory of theirs.

Until he explained this to me in my late teens, I thought the photograph was of *his* hands: they were certainly similar. He was hurt (and I was ashamed) to think I could have supposed him capable of such vanity.

While he was learning the intricacies of his trade at the hands of Victor Bonney, I was having the first lesson in mine. As he with his stethoscope was listening to the pulse of the heart, I was listening to the pulse of the voice. My mother was a singer good enough to perform on the radio in New Zealand. She sang like a blackbird, instinctively, with a voice pure, simple, and strong. She sang me the nursery rhymes her mother had sung her, giving me my first taste of poetry, a taste like any other that we enjoy long before we understand *what* we're enjoying. Nursery rhymes make their first impact − like much other poetry − with their music, and their music is more intricate than is often supposed:

> I had a little *nut*-tree, *noth*ing would it bear
> *But* a silver *nut*-meg and a golden pear;
> The King of Spain's daughter came to visit me,
> And all for the sake of my little *nut*-tree.

The internal rhymes, the chiming vowels (*daughter/all*, Sp*ain/sake*), the alliterating *b*s and *s*s, not to mention the repetition of the first and last lines, produce a texture of woven sounds that has delighted children for two hundred years. What is the magic in such spells? T.S. Eliot famously said that 'the ghost of some simple metre should lurk behind the arras in even the "freest" verse; to advance menacingly as we doze, and withdraw as we rouse'. Certainly, that principle is at work in 'I had a little nut-tree'. If we replace the delicate movement of the ghost with a policeman's tread, the magic vanishes:

> I had a little nut-tree, nothing would it bear
> *Except* a silver nut-meg and a golden pear . . .

My mother knew nothing of the terms of English prosody, but she sang me the march of the iamb:

> O, the **grand** old **Duke** of **York**,
> He **had** ten **thou**sand **men**;
> He **marched** them **up** . . .

(here the soldiers broke step into three sprightly syncopated anapests)

> to the **top** of the **hill**
> And he **marched** them **down** again!

She sang me skipping trochees – '**Polly put** the **ket**tle **on**' – and cantering dactyls:

> **Ride** a cock-**horse** to **Ban**bury **Cross**,
> To **see** a fine **lad**y up**on** a white **horse**;
> With **rings** on her **fing**ers and **bells** on her **toes**,
> **She** shall have **mus**ic wher**ev**er she **goes**.

I can see and hear now that the particular charm of many nursery rhymes derives from their expressive magic, language imitating action:

> **Hump**ty **Dump**ty **sat** on a **wall**;
> **Hump**ty **Dump**ty **had** a great **fall**;
> **All** the king's **hors**es and **all** the king's **men**
> **Couldn't** put **Hump**ty **Dump**ty to**geth**er a**gain**.

The cadence of the last line is as fractured as Humpty Dumpty. Similarly:

> **Jack** and **Jill** went **up** the **hill**
> To **fetch** a **pail** of **wat**er;
> **Jack** fell **down** and **broke** his **crown**,
> And **Jill** came **tumb**ling **aft**er.

The trudging alternation of trochaic and iambic lines is strikingly interrupted by the ghostly extra syllable in 'tumbling' that mimics Jill's head-over-heels descent.

In all of these rhymes, the primitive poet (like his successors) achieves his effect by setting up a pattern of expectation and then giving his listeners not what they expect but a surprising variation. Again, the anonymous rhymer tells us our first stories, introducing us to the pleasures of narrative and its representation of direct and indirect speech. His rhymes stick like burrs in the memory – well before we know what the words mean – and cling there longer than most experiences of childhood.

Like any other mother, mine as the months passed began to explain the words, admitting me to a secondary world of kings and queens, cobblers and drummers, candles and cradles, ploughs and carts, a world very different from our own in the 1930s. Her singing and her explanations introduced me to an English past, largely rural and inhabited by animals not to be seen in Kew Gardens or in the streets and shops of South London. This secondary world would become the world of my imagination.

Repetition is of the essence of the nursery rhyme: the words repeated, the refrain, and the fact that it is spoken or sung time after time. I hadn't inherited my mother's ear for music, couldn't hold in my head the sequence of notes in a vertical scale, but from the start I had a sense of rhythm, the sequence of stresses on a horizontal scale. As she sang her nursery rhymes, increasingly I would accompany her, beating out the rhythm with a grubby hand or a wooden spoon.

There was soon to be a second singer in the family. Life in the Mortlake Road flat had been complicated by Jemima's theft of our only clock. Then one day my father came home from work and asked my mother to look out of the window:

'What do you see that wasn't there this morning?'

'There's a parked car.'

'It's ours.'

'You haven't bought a *car!*'

'No,' he said, 'it's a clock with a car round it.'

With his bank manager's help, he had bought a venerable Singer in which, the following summer, he drove us to Scotland to meet the Scottish Howies. The highlight of that expedition was a gathering of the clan at which he was conscious of being closely observed by a spinster schoolmistress, who finally plucked up courage to ask him a Personal Question:

'You aren't a *full-blooded* Maori, are you?'

'No,' he replied, 'not *full*-blooded.'

In 1937, at Victor Bonney's prompting, he and my mother embarked on a more major expedition: he to study the work of some notable German surgeons in Berlin and Vienna, then the Mecca and Medina of the surgical world. The Singer and I were left at home, the one parked in Mortlake Road, the other in the Norland Nursery staffed by starched ladies who crackled as they walked.

My father always said he learnt a great deal in Germany, but his most enduring memory was of a curious breach of medical etiquette (whereby a surgeon, if his patient dies on the table, traditionally abandons the operation). I heard him tell the story – and he was a good story-teller – many times over the years that followed, years that gave the incident greater significance. Only when the war was over did I understand it, and it was some years after that that I stole it for a poem:

A Letter from Berlin

> *My dear,*
> 　　*Today a letter from Berlin*
> *where snow – the first of '38 – flew in,*
> *settled and shrivelled on the lamp last night,*
> *broke moth wings mobbing the window. Light*
> *woke me early, but the trams were late:*
> *I had to run from the Brandenburg Gate*
> *skidding, groaning like a tram, and sodden*
> *to the knees. Von Neumann operates at 10*
> *and would do if the sky fell in. They lock*
> *his theatre doors on the stroke of the clock –*
> *but today I was lucky: found a gap*
> *in the gallery next to a chap*
> *I knew just as the doors were closing. Last,*
> *as expected, on Von Showmann's list*
> *the new vaginal hysterectomy*
> *that brought me to Berlin.*
> 　　　　　　　　　　*Delicately*
> *he went to work, making from right to left*
> *a semi-circular incision. Deft*
> *dissection of the fascia. The blood-*

blossoming arteries nipped in the bud.
Speculum, scissors, clamps — the uterus
cleanly delivered, the pouch of Douglas
stripped to the rectum, and the cavity
closed. Never have I seen such masterly
technique, 'And so little bleeding!' I said
half to myself, half to my neighbour.

                                   'Dead',
came his whisper. 'Don't be a fool'
I said, for still below us in the pool
of light the marvellous unhurried hands
were stitching, tying the double strands
of catgut, stitching, tying. It was like
a concert, watching those hands unlock
the music from their score. And at the end
one half expected him to turn and bend
stiffly towards us. Stiffly he walked out
and his audience shuffled after. But
finishing my notes in the gallery
I saw them uncover the patient: she
was dead.

               I met my neighbour in the street
waiting for the same tram, stamping his feet
on the pavement's broken snow, and said:
'I have to apologize. She was dead,
but how did you know?' Back came his voice
like a bullet '— saw it last month, twice.'

Returning your letter to an envelope
yellower by years than when you sealed it up,
darkly the omens emerge. A ritual wound
yellow at the lip yawns in my hand;
a turbulent crater; a trench, filled
not with snow only, east of Buchenwald.

The war was still a dark cloud massing over Europe when, in
1938, my father applied for a job as first assistant to Professor
Moir, head of the Oxford University Department of Obstetrics

and Gynaecology, and was appointed. We moved to a small upstairs flat in North Oxford, where we were joined for a crowded month by my father's parents and younger sister. Of this, I remember only one – painful – moment: my grandfather shutting the Singer door on my right hand. The pain is not now in my hand, but in the face with the sad mouth under a white moustache, a face lashed by my father's outburst of anguish and fury: 'It's his *right* hand!'

After my grandparents had returned to New Zealand, we moved again, to Woodstock Close, a red-brick barrack-like block of flats at the outer edge of the city's intellighetto. Ours was a small flat, up fifty-three wooden stairs, overlooking pleasant lawns flanked by trees. I had a room to myself, with a blood-red map above the bed.

★

Every morning, my mother would walk me up the Woodstock Road to the Wayside Nursery School and, every afternoon, walk me home. Memory knocks on that door, but it doesn't open. After her death, I found among my mother's papers a carefully preserved sheaf of reports. These show that 4-year-old Waysiders were introduced to sixteen subjects – from Arithmetic to Writing, by way of Oral Composition and Poetry, Spelling and Story – but even those scrupulously annotated menu cards bring back no memories of what was set before us, perched on our benches in linen smocks like small peasants at a harvest supper. I see that in my final term the Story was 'Hiawatha' – probably a prose retelling of Longfellow's Red Indian epic, but I like to think we would have been given a taste of the original:

> Swift of foot was Hiawatha:
> He could shoot an arrow from him,
> And run forward with such fleetness,
> That the arrow fell behind him!

I remember, however, what my mother read me after we had walked home. We had almost no books in the flat, other than medical textbooks, and she had to ask my teacher what to read me and what I should be starting to read myself. The answer was 'Beatrix Potter', so she bought a copy of *Peter Rabbit* and we read it together, side by side. To be more precise, for the first umpteen times *she* read the little block of text on each left-hand page while *I* 'read' the picture on the right. When I had exhausted the imaginative possibilities of the picture, I turned my attention to the mysteries on the left and began to learn their cadences – long before I could relate them to the black signs on the page. We played a game: she would leave out a word – and later a sentence – and I would be expected to pounce and supply it. Soon I could fit the sound to the sight of some shorter words and was relishing the 'taste' of longer ones:

> Peter gave himself up for lost, and shed big tears; but his sobs were overheard by some friendly sparrows, who flew to him in great excitement, and implored him to exert himself.

I particularly liked 'implored' and 'exert' (which would probably now be edited out of a book for young children) and played with them as with a new toy; asking my father when, at the end of a day, he thundered into the flat with a gust of laughter and ether: 'Did you exert yourself today?' I was always better at remembering the sound of a word than its meaning. So, when my father was showing a New Zealand friend round Oxford, and the tall stranger asked 'What's *your* favourite college, son?' I couldn't think why they both laughed when I said 'Gynaecollege'.

My mother's advisers guided her on from Beatrix Potter to Alison Uttley and Jean de Brunhof, and I was soon familiar with the ways of rabbits, hares, hedgehogs, frogs, owls, elephants, and many other occupants of Noah's Ark that I had never seen in the flesh, feathers, or fur, but knew to have domestic lives very like our own. Then the advisers recommended A.A. Milne and I was introduced to Christopher Robin and *his* menagerie. We didn't warm to each other, and my mother and I moved on to Milne's *When We Were Very Young*. I liked his poems much more than *Winnie-the-Pooh*. Two in particular seemed to enter the memory without being memorized and were very good for chanting, the first 'The King's Breakfast', because of its 'chain-linked' rhetorical structure:

> The King asked
> The Queen, and
> The Queen asked
> The Dairymaid:
> 'Could we have some butter for
> The Royal slice of bread?'
> The Queen asked
> The Dairymaid,
> The Dairymaid
> Said, 'Certainly,
> I'll go and tell
> The cow
> Now
> Before she goes to bed.'
>
> The Dairymaid
> She curtsied,
> And went and told
> The Alderney:
> 'Don't forget the butter for
> The Royal slice of bread.'
> The Alderney
> Said sleepily:
> 'You'd better tell
> His Majesty
> That many people nowadays
> Like marmalade
> Instead.'

The links of the chain are now reversed, as the Cow's word is passed from Dairymaid to Queen to King; and then reversed again, as the King's word is passed back down the chain to the Cow, who relents, and her word and butter are passed – fast – back to the King:

> The Queen took
> The butter
> And brought it to
> His Majesty;
> The King said,
> 'Butter, eh?'
> And bounced out of bed.
> 'Nobody,' he said,
> As he kissed her
> Tenderly,
> 'Nobody,' he said
> As he slid down
> The banisters,
> 'Nobody,
> My darling,
> Could call me
> A fussy man –
> BUT
> *I do like a little bit of butter to my bread!'*

Very different from this free verse (with the bed/said/bread rhyme that 'locks up' each paragraph) was the formal structure of my other favourite, 'Bad Sir Brian Botany':

Sir Brian had a battleaxe with great big knobs on;
    He went among the villagers and blipped them on the head.
On Wednesday and on Saturday, but mostly on the latter day,
    He called at all the cottages, and this is what he said:

> 'I am Sir Brian!' (*ting-ling*)
>   'I am Sir Brian!' (*rat-tat*)
>   'I am Sir Brian, as bold as a lion –
>   Take *that!* – and *that!* – and *that!*'

The alternating quatrains of narrative and refrain look and sound very different, but are cunningly related by the four strong stresses that structure each line. I delighted in the story, so fluidly unfolded through these strict stanzas, of Sir Brian's public ducking by outraged villagers and his penitent rehabilitation:

> Sir Brian struggled home again, and chopped up his battleaxe,
>> Sir Brian took his fighting boots, and threw them on the fire.
> He is quite a different person now he hasn't got his spurs on,
>> And he goes about the village as B. Botany, Esquire.

>> 'I am Sir Brian? Oh, *no*!
>>> I am Sir Brian? Who's he?
>> *I* haven't got any title, I'm Botany –
>>> Plain Mr Botany (B).'

When we moved on to Milne's *Now We Are Six*, a developing taste for Romance in faraway times and climes led me to enjoy the company of 'The Knight whose Armour didn't Squeak' – another story appropriately encased in rivetted rhyme and metre – and 'The Old Sailor', whose opening lines suggest he might have been one of the children of the old woman who lived in a shoe:

> There was once an old sailor my grandfather knew
> Who had so many things which he wanted to do
> That, whenever he thought it was time to begin,
> He couldn't because of the state he was in.

I like to think part of my pleasure in the indecisions of the ship-wrecked sailor may have been due to an ingenious metrical joke (only later perceived): the fact that this story of a man incapable of action is told in cantering dactyls, the most active of metres:

> And so in the end he did nothing at all,
> But basked on the shingle wrapped up in a shawl.
> And I think it was dreadful the way he behaved –
> He did nothing but basking until he was saved!

There's much that can be said against Milne's verse – the sometimes cloying sentiment, the metrical expectations invariably fulfilled – but the inventive variety of its stanza forms makes it a useful bridge between nursery rhymes and poetry proper.

While I was crossing that bridge in 1940, I was only dimly aware that unfunny knights and sailors were in action in a world of which the BBC's Nine O'clock News brought my parents a report each evening after I had gone to bed. My friend Rory gave me a useful lesson when I visited his flat, at the other end of our building, and asked him who was the man in the mantle-piece photo. I liked his face – and his cross-belt. He said it was his father, an officer in the Argyll and Sutherland Highlanders. I asked him where he was. He said he had been captured by the Germans and was in a prisoner-of-war camp. I was chilled. The possibility that this could happen to *my* father filled me with anxiety, and that evening I asked him if it could. No, he said. He had tried to join the army, but they wouldn't let him. There was no work for a woman's doctor in the army. So I went to sleep under my blood-red map, happily unaware that half the maps of Europe had blood on them; my only worry, whether I would learn to write well enough to go to the Dragon School, where they had a sandpit.

2

Mythology and History

AT LAST: the hushed nave of Sts Elliston and Cavell, outfitters by appointment to the Dragon School. Ahead of us, the mothers of two older boys were talking:

'How many marks did you get for *your* Latin prose?'

'Seven.'

'I got five for mine.'

I didn't hear the exchange – being absorbed in the iconography of blazer pockets – and didn't understand it when it was reported to my father that evening.

'What's a Latin prose?'

My mother – whose knowledge of Latin I would later discover extended no further than *impedimentum*, neuter, a baggage-animal – retired to the kitchen at this point, leaving the explanation to him. Apparently, Latin was a language like English, but older. Those were Latin words on the pocket of the new navy-blue blazer I was showing off. So taken was I with the yellow dragon, tongue of flame licking the icecream-like section of sun, that I hadn't thought to ask what the words meant.

'*Arduus ad Solem*,' he said, 'which means' (his memory groping back past his medical Latin to that of his Auckland Grammar School days) 'it's difficult to reach the sun.'

★

Mother and father

On May Morning 1941, my mother walked me down Bardwell Road (only later would I notice the happy associations of that name) to the Dragon School for the first time. The dragon on my pocket was a comfort, but I was feeling more naked than armoured as I crossed the threshold of the bottom form of the Baby School. I was still alive, however, and even jubilant, when she came to collect me at 12.30.

Was I then, or at any time in the months ahead, aware of the tongues of flame melting the walls of London and the bodies of Londoners fifty miles to the south-east? I don't think so. At 6 o'clock every evening, she would turn the bakelite knob on our wireless and listen to the well-bred voice from behind the little grille. If I listened at all, I knew that nothing I need worry about could be said so calmly. I did, sometime later, overhear my parents talking of an American offer to take Oxford children into their homes 'for the duration'. I listened to that, because it seemed an alarming possibility and already several of my contemporaries had vanished, like the Pied Piper's flock into the mountain. My alarm was momentary, as I heard my father say: 'No, we'll sink or swim together' (though I only understood the 'No').

I was more interested in mythology than history, and particularly the mythology of my new surroundings. The school, it was said, had been founded by a ship's captain – known as the Skipper – and named after his yacht (surely at least a schooner), the *Blue Dragon*. He had sailed the Seven Seas and been lowered to his last resting place in one of them. Resemblance to family mythology – voyages out to New Zealand under sail, back under steam, rounding the Horn in mid-winter – predisposed me to think well of the Skipper and his ship (probably a brigantine), the *Blue Dragon*.

In due course, but not for some years, I learnt the difference between mythology and history, the second no less rewarding than the first.

It appeared that, in 1877, a Government Commission on the Universities recommended that the Fellows of colleges should be released from their medieval rule of celibacy and allowed to marry. Heads of colleges had long been exempt from this prohibition, and the implementation of the Commission's recommendation enabled a number of Oxford college Fellows to make honest men of themselves and honest women of those they had installed in charming houses discreetly set some way back from the Woodstock Road. The extent to which the government was authorizing the closing of the stable door after the horse had bolted is revealed by the fact that in the very same year, 1877, a group of thirty Oxford dons set up a 'Visiting Council' to organize and oversee a school for their sons. This, known at first as 'The Oxford Preparatory School', opened its doors that September to fourteen boys, mostly sons of the founding fathers, including that of H.G. Liddell, Dean of Christ Church. If young Lionel Charles Liddell's experiences at the school were less bizarre than his sister Alice's recent adventures in Wonderland, there have been those who have wondered whether some of the school's subsequent eccentricities were not inspired by Lewis Carroll.

The riddle of How the Dragon Got its Name was answered, sixty years after the event, by another of the founding sons, Clement Rogers, who wrote:

It must have been in the second term when our numbers were growing that it was thought we ought to play football. A ball was provided and a ground found for us, a field behind No. 1 South Parks Road, now part of the grounds of Mansfield College.

The first game was not a great success. There was no one to coach us and we had only vague ideas about the rules, so the game chiefly consisted of argument and soon petered out. So we foregathered under a tree to discuss things.

I, like the rest, was about twelve years old at the time. Now I had for some time, probably since the summer holidays when my brothers came home from school, wanted to be a 'member of a club'. It was partly the desire to be with others, and I had now got that at school. But the chief thing I wanted was to wear the outward signs of club membership in the form of a polo cap and a badge. The blue polo cap I had, but without a badge it signified nothing. Someone else suggested our forming ourselves into a club. We all agreed, and I saw the opportunity of realising my longed-for ideal.

The first question was, of course, what we should call ourselves. With a badge in mind I made a suggestion. Our family crest was a heron, and the club of my imagination had always been the Heron Club, so I suggested that we should call ourselves 'The Herons'. The suggestion met with no favour. 'Why Herons?' they asked, and I could not give the real reason.

Suggestions were being made which met with no great approval, and I hastily cast about in my mind for another idea. I had heard that there was a 'Governing Body' of the School, and one of them was a Mr George, a Fellow of New College. I thought of the gold sovereigns then in currency with the figure of St George and the Dragon on the back. So I suggested, 'There's a Mr George who is one of the governors or something. Let's be the Dragons.' And Dragons we were from that moment.

Then came the great question of the badge. The meeting was all alive. Some of us had sisters who did needlework. 'I believe my sister could do some dragons to wear on our caps,' said one, 'I'll ask her.' 'I'll ask mine too', said another, and in a day or two the results were appearing. The work was well meaning but amateurish. Still, we were none of us critical and we got our people to sew them on.

We had done it all ourselves. We wore our Dragons proudly, and they soon attracted the notice of Mr Clarke [the Headmaster]. We explained their significance. He was kind, and made no comment on their artistic deficiencies, but said there should be uniformity. He would see that someone was found, professionally skilled in the art of embroidery, who, for a reasonable sum, would provide us with standardised Dragons.

This was official recognition, given by Authority. The title and badge had received, so to speak, the Royal Assent, and I felt proud at having been the humble instrument in suggesting the name, though I little realised the extent of the recognition it was to receive in future days.

In 1886, the Headmaster died and was succeeded by the assistant he had appointed five years before, young Mr C.C. Lynam. This was the mythic Ancient Mariner. Joining the staff of the OPS, he commissioned the building of a 'canoe-yawl', the

Skipper and son, Sound of Mull, 1934

Snake, which he raced with some success at the Falmouth Regatta and on the Norfolk Broads. From this he graduated to a centre-board sloop – painted yellow and christened the *Yellow Dragon* – which was wrecked off the North Norfolk coast in August 1891. The Skipper (as he was now known) then commissioned the building of his first *Blue Dragon*: 'Yawl-rigged, registered 7 tons at Lloyds, 25 feet over all, 20 feet water-line, beam 9 feet, draft 2 feet 9, and 5 feet with plate down; no fo'csle but one large cabin.'

Legend proclaims him a great sailor and a great schoolmaster, whose relaxed style is engagingly exemplified by the story of a later *Blue Dragon* – there were to be three – that went to the bottom of Oban Harbour in a storm. With her went all the previous term's school bills and reports, a problem the Skipper solved by writing to every parent: 'Your boy is doing splendidly. Please pay what you think you owe.'

There was truth in the legend that he died at sea – but aboard a Blue Funnel Line steamer rather than a *Blue Dragon*. He had taken his leave of the school like Tennyson's 'Ulysses', who in one of the Skipper's favourite poems had said 'I cannot rest from travel':

> On the morning of October 20th [1938] he was at the Hymn in the Old Hall to say goodbye to the boys. He told them he was taking their Holiday Diaries with him. He said he was sailing on board the *Alcinous*, and after telling them about Alcinous and Ulysses, and quoting from Kipling's 'Mandalay' about being shipped 'somewhere East of Suez', he asked for an 'extra half', said goodbye and then made his way down the Hall through a crowd of cheering boys, one of whom slipped a late Diary under his arm.

He was 80 years old and had always said he wanted to die and be buried at sea. His wish was granted, a week later, ten miles north of Cape Bon in the Mediterranean.

★

My mythological and historical interests soon found a focus outside the school. Remembering perhaps my pleasure in A.A. Milne's 'The Knight whose Armour didn't Squeak' and 'Bad Sir Brian Botany', my mother bought me *Stories of King Arthur's Knights/told to the Children by Mary MacGregor*, which again we read together. Intoxicated by my first taste of Malory, I signalled my identification with his spotless heroes by defacing the flyleaf with the signature of a dyslexic spider. I liked best the stories of 'Gareth and Lynette' and 'The Death of King Arthur', my imagination fired by their colour plates of 'brave knights and fair ladies' painted in a highly stylized Pre-Raphaelite mode.

Soon I was day-dreaming of rescuing fair ladies and dispatching their craven captors with a back-hand from my trusty blade but, in my first test of this kind, I failed miserably.

One morning, my mother and I were walking down the Banbury Road when we heard shouts on the other side and saw a stationary coal-cart on the back of which the coal-heaver was flogging his 'boy'. The man was huge (at least to my 6-year-old eyes) and as black as the Black Knight killed by the good Gareth. His belt buckle flashed in the sunlight over the howling boy.

'Stay here and DON'T MOVE!' said my mother – borrowing what should have been *my* line – in a voice of fierce authority I hadn't heard before. Rooted to the spot, I watched in horror as she ran across the road, hitched up her skirt, clambered on to the cart, and seized the Black Knight's arm. Clearly, he was about to kill her in front of her own knight, who stood spellbound across the street. There was more shouting, but suddenly I realized that the voice was hers, telling the coal-heaver what she thought of him. Disarmed (she had thrown his belt into the gutter) and dejected, his shoulders sagging under their black leather armour, he was reduced to muttering 'Yes'm . . . no mum'.

She jumped lightly off the cart, trotted across the road, took my hand and, saying nothing, marched me down the street.

My second knightly test I failed also.

My father had a surgeon friend who kept a sailing dinghy in Chichester Harbour and invited us to join him one weekend. Primed with the Skipper myth and my parents' talk of rounding the Horn in mid-winter, I liked the sound of this expedition – rather more than I liked my first sight of the very small boat and the very large sea. It was mid-afternoon and a stiff wind was blowing as we hoisted sail and headed out of the harbour. Our skipper (with a small s) explained the importance of a disciplined crew crossing from one side of the boat to the other every time she 'went about', and soon we were providing a good counterweight to the straining mainsail. My initial unease had long since changed to exhilaration when suddenly the dinghy gybed, the boom swung across with a sickening crack, and we capsized. My mother had a firm hold of my belt as we went over, and I think the mast must have broken because the boat was not on its side but upside down, and the four of us were clinging to the upturned hull.

My mother said something about 'an adventure', and remembering how the *real* Skipper had been many times shipwrecked, I began to feel quite cheerful. Another boat, they said, was bound to pick us up in a few minutes, but no other boats were out and late afternoon gave place to early evening.

It was then that I saw the knights – a great cloud company of them – moving majestically along the western horizon. They were wearing colourful coat-armour, the plumes of their helmets streamed behind them, and their horses were richly caparisoned. It didn't occur to me to ask if they were real, but in some important sense I believed in them and they engrossed my attention as the hours passed.

My father, meanwhile, seeing that the tide had turned and we were being carried out to sea, said he would try to swim ashore. As soon as he let go of the boat, however, the trapped air that was keeping her afloat began to bubble from the gunwale and the others called him back. (In the event, this was fortunate because, even if he had been able to swim the considerable distance to the shore, he could never have crossed the mudflats exposed by the receding tide.) When, I suspect, the other members of the crew had all but given up hope of rescue, a dinghy put out from a fishing boat anchored inshore and one by one we were hauled, exhausted, into it.

The fisherman had been working in his engine-room when his 4-year-old son had called down to him that 'funny people were in the water'. At first he took no notice, but when the boy repeated it, he came up to look. The 4-year-old was the hero of the hour, and my father later bought him a toy crane as a present. I felt more than a twinge of envy at both his hero status and his crane, but my sharpest memory of that salt-water baptism remains the stately cavalcade on the western horizon.

Heroes (ancient and modern) and knights were much discussed at the Dragon School. There was talk of them in the playground and from time to time in the twenty-minute classes in which we were taught Reading, Poetry, Writing, Spelling, Arithmetic, and Other Subjects – to follow the order (I have always assumed of importance) in which they appeared on our reports. These forms were brought round and handed out by the headmaster, A.E. ('Hum') Lynam, every week. Younger brother of the legendary Skipper, he was in his late sixties and had already handed over much of the day-to-day running of the school to the next member of the Lynam dynasty, his own son Joc. Hum had the air of an old English sheepdog and his brother's skill in directing his flock. Like his brother, he had decided views about Poetry, which he held to be a prime – perhaps *the* prime – repository of the English-speaking people's culture and history. Children should therefore be taught to enjoy it, which, in his view, meant learning reams of it by heart. More than that, they should learn to speak it – both for the intrinsic pleasure of *hearing* it and as a first lesson in 'public-speaking', which he considered a vital skill.

In our twenty-minute poetry lessons, then, the form mistress would tell us about a poem, read it aloud, and assign us each a few lines to be learnt at home and recited in class next day. At the end of term, every child in the Baby School was required to recite a poem in front of the headmaster's nodding white head and twitching moustache. So I came to be acquainted with Eugene Field's 'Wynken, Blynken, and Nod'. In a copy of *The Golden Staircase* (Part 2),

> Wynken, Blynken and Nod one night
> Sailed off in a wooden shoe –
> Sailed on a river of crystal light,
> Into a sea of dew.

These seem now the first words I ever really heard: not over-heard, like my mother's nursery rhymes, but heard inside the head, syllable by syllable, reverberant, a plucked string. No matter that I had no idea who Wynken, Blynken and Nod might be, or what 'crystal' might mean. Enough that the words seemed alive, a spell filling my head with a new happiness by day, singing me to sleep at night.

Poetry was not the only compensation for the unequal strug-gle with arithmetic: there was the sandpit at bun-break and, on Tuesday and Thursday afternoons, there were games on the big field of the Big School. That first summer there was racing and jumping and in the autumn, better still, there was football. When I told my father of this important development, of the two teams of eleven forwards (no goalkeeper) scoring freely with six balls, he asked me what shape they were.

'Shape?'

'Yes.'

'They're footballs, they're round.'

He looked thoughtful and said he'd come to watch us next week, which he did, and the following day told me he'd brought me a present. His right hand was behind his back. When he whipped it round, it held a leather object, laced like a football but more the shape of a vegetable marrow. This, he explained, was a *rugger* ball, what *New Zealanders* played football with. Together we ran down the stairs to the lawn, where he kicked it into the air for me to catch. This was the first of many such ses-sions. Whenever he was home before sunset, out we would go with the ball, which soon assumed the mysterious – even magical – properties of a tribal fetish. Running together, he in his hospital suit and shiny shoes, we would pass it between us or set it free to dance ahead of us. And when it became as indistinct as the circling bats, we would thunder up the stairs again to supper and another lesson in history and mythology: his stories of New Zealand's invincible All Blacks.

Sometime later, the same concern for tribal values, physical skills to counterbalance the Poetry, History, and Mythology of Bardwell Road, led him to announce I was to learn to ride. It was then that he told me of delivering his father's newspapers on horseback which, reinforcing my interest in knights and cowboys, made me eager to start.

One Sunday afternoon, we walked down to Port Meadow, a three-hundred-acre field to the north of Oxford, and I was introduced to the strangest old woman I had ever met. Miss Lavender looked like a witch and spoke like an Oxford don. She had straw in her hair and horse-dung on her tattered mac. My father liked her, because she cared for and understood her horses as he did his patients, and she and her shaggy familiars certainly made an impact on me:

> Miss Lavender taught us to ride
> clamping halfcrowns between saddle and knee
> on Sunday afternoons
> in a watermeadow one mile wide:
> and the hot halfcrowns
> she would keep, after an hour, for her fee.
>
> Her horses stepped like a king's own
> always to imperatives of Spanish drill.
> Miss Lavender said,
> 'A horseman has to be thrown
> ten times.' From thoroughbred
> to exploding grass we headoverheeled; until
>
> that March the watermeadow froze
> and Miss Lavender died, consumptive
> on a stable floor
> among motionless horses. Those
> died after for no reason, or
> for want of a Spanish imperative.

I was teased at school about my riding. The fact that I was taught by an old woman who looked like a witch proved it was a sissy sport for girls. I countered with talk of cowboys and knights, and my Sunday afternoons were generally agreed to be an allowable eccentricity. I was, after all, a foreigner of sorts, a role I sometimes resented, sometimes rejoiced in. I could see it had advantages: for one thing, I had no nanny. My parents, on principle, would never have employed one, even if they could have afforded it. At my friends' birthday parties, therefore, I was the only boy without a starched spectre at his back, waiting to twist his ear like the key of a Hornby engine if he misbehaved.

I returned from one such occasion in high good humour, saying I'd had three jellies.

'You ate *three* jellies?'

'No, I ate two.'

'What happened to the third?'

'I threw it at Kenneth.'

Kenneth Moir was my host and the son of my father's Professor. I was not invited to his party the following year, because (so my father heard) I was said to be 'incorrigible'. He and my mother had no more idea what 'incorrigible' meant than I did and they had to look it up in the dictionary.

Our situations were not dissimilar: they too were Colonials unaccustomed to the ways, and particularly the coded circumlocutions, of the British middle class. My father too was thought to be something of a Wild Colonial Boy. He spoke his mind and did everything fast: he operated fast and drove fast (for sixty years without an accident). He drove like a surgeon, watching the road with unwavering concentration, listening to the murmur of the Rover 20 that had by now replaced his asthmatic Singer as to a foetal heart. His car was always his one indulgence and his favourite instrument, and none was ever more favoured than the midnight-blue 'drophead coupé' he had bought for a song and looked after like a patient. On a Saturday morning, if he wasn't delivering a baby or opening an abdomen, he would have opened the burnished bonnet and be cleaning or oiling its spotless organs.

Early in the war, ambulances being scarce, he set up a Flying

Edmund Blunden, drawn by William Rothenstein, 1922

Squad to respond to obstetrical emergencies in the countryside around Oxford. A young doctor with a fast car was always on call. It proved a great success, and the model for many other such units, despite an initial setback.

One of my father's colleagues, anxious to improve on his record time from Oxford to Rugby, accelerated up a little hill only to find it a hump-backed bridge. Drinkers in the Boat Inn heard the roar of an engine, the rush of tyres, then – for a long moment – just the engine, and finally a rending crash. The drinkers rushed out to see, in the beam of the landlord's torch, a lopsided car with a broken back axle, two slumped bodies inside, and, welling out of it, a terrible dark stain. An ambulance was called, but before it arrived a miracle occurred: the bodies stirred, groaned, and climbed out. The doctor and nurse, in addition to mild concussion, had lost twelve pints of blood (in bottles on the back seat). History does not record the fate of the woman to whose emergency they were responding.

For my father and mother, the most important obstetrical event – indeed, the most important event – of 1942 was the birth of twin daughters. It was an event that would transform our family life, but not – in the short term – have much effect on my 'writerly' life. My sisters Sally and Wendy brought much happiness with them, not only radiating from their small persons, but also resulting from a necessary move to a larger flat. This was on a lower floor of our red-brick barracks, and its delights included a balcony and (for me) a poet for a neighbour, the first poet I ever knowingly saw, Edmund Blunden. I don't think we ever exchanged a word, but the small dark man became for a small dark boy the *genius loci* of Woodstock Close.

3

Latin

AS MY FAMILY moved down, I moved up, into the Big School, joining the herd corralled at Assembly in the cavernous Old Hall. The headmasters stood on a dais: the white-headed Hum mumbled a few words; his son Joc barked a few more, then smiled like a shark, and announced a hymn. Two hundred and fifty battered copies of *Hymns and Prayers for Dragons* fluttered like a wood in a wind. A piano thumped out the opening bars of 'Onward Christian Soldiers' and we were off. Then, having finished 'marching as to war', we stampeded into the playground for fifteen minutes of Drill. We paraded under the command of 'Colonel' Purnell, a veteran of the Boer War (with scars to prove it, even if his rank owed more to rhyme than military history). You couldn't imagine him – bald head, wire-rimmed specs, long khaki shorts – relieving the Siege of Mafeking, and his Drill was of the 'arms bend, knees stretch' variety. On mornings when his contingent was more than usually sleepy, he would preface some of his orders with 'O'Grady says'. These were to be ignored, but someone always fell into the trap, earning the Colonel's comic tirade.

At the command 'Dismiss!' we headed for our classrooms and the daily ration of a Dragon's staple diet. Latin.

★

'Before we start, we'd better agree what it is we're starting on. What *is* Latin?'

'Please, sir, my father says it's a dead language.'

'It's certainly a language. The language spoken by the ancient Romans living in a place called Latium in Italy. But what did your father mean when he said it was dead?'

'He didn't say.'

'What does your father do?'

'He works in a bank.'

'So he works with money.'

'Yes.'

'Do you have any money on you?'

'Yes, I've got some pennies.'

'Would you please write what you've got on the black-board?'

Matthews took the piece of chalk and wrote a large *3d*.

'Good. What does the *d* stand for?'

'I don't know.'

'Does anyone know?' No one did. 'It stands for *denarius*, the Latin word for a small coin. What's written on your pennies?' Matthews scowled at them.

'It says GEORGIUS V DEI GRA:BRITT:OMN:REX FID: DEF: IND:IMP:'

'What does that mean?'

'I don't know.'

'Does anyone know?' No one did. 'It stands for George the Fifth, *dei gratia* (by God's grace) *Brittanniae Omnis* (of all Britain) *Rex* (King) *Fidei Defensor* (Defender of the Faith) *Indiae Imperator* (Emperor of India). Thank you, Matthews. You can sit down.

'When Matthews' father said Latin was a *dead* language, he was right in the sense that no one speaks it or writes it all the time – as they did in the days of the Roman Empire. But in another sense, it's still *alive* and all around us: used on our coins, used by lawyers, used by doctors, used by Roman Catholics, used by anyone who speaks English, since so many English words are borrowed from Latin. Just about all the great English writers were brought up on Latin, learning their craft from the great Latin writers. If you want to understand those great writers of your own language properly, if you want to write like them, you'll need to know Latin, too.'

★

The catch was that, to learn Latin, you had to learn Latin grammar. It didn't occur to us to ask how it was we had learnt English without learning English grammar. So far, grammar had escaped our attention, or *we* had escaped *its* attention. If we knew of it at all, it was as some sort of mythical beast, but now it was snapping at our heels every day from 9.30 to 11.00 (when everyone in the Big School did Latin, except those in the upper forms who did Greek). In Kennedy's *Revised Latin Primer* we were introduced to

PARTS OF SPEECH

Words are classified **as**:

I. **Nouns** (or **Substantives**), names of persons, places, things, or qualities:

Caesar, *Caesar*; **Rōma**, *Rome*; **sōl**, *sun*; **fortitūdō**, *bravery*.

II. **Adjectives**, which define nouns by expressing their qualities:
Rōma **antīqua**, *ancient Rome*; sōl **clārus**, *the bright sun*.

III. **Pronouns**, which point out a person, place, thing, or quality without naming it:

ego, *I*; **ille**, *that, he*.

IV. **Verbs**, which express an action or state:
Sōl **dat** lūcem, *the sun gives light*; Rōma **manet**, *Rome remains*.

V. **Adverbs**, which qualify and limit Verbs, Adjectives, and sometimes other Adverbs:

Rōma **diū** flōruit; nunc **minus** potens est.
Rome flourished long; now it is less powerful.

Even in these 'scales' can be detected the key notes of subsequent imperial marches and symphonies. At first, the notes are separate: *Caesar; Rome; sun; bravery*. Then the subtextual metaphor begins to emerge: *ancient Rome; the bright sun*. It emerges explicitly: *the sun gives light; Rome remains*; before becoming implicit: *Rome flourished long; now it is less powerful*. The imperial sun has passed its zenith.

We, with *sol* still blazing on our blazers, didn't know – and our teachers may not have known – that our curriculum had been shaped by imperial priorities. It was no accident that the expansion of the British public school in the second half of the nineteenth century coincided with the expansion of the British Empire: the role of the one was to provide proconsuls for the other. Rome was the model and Latin the means whereby its values were transmitted. Dr Arnold, architect of the nineteenth-century public school, had written a *History of Rome*, and Lord Macaulay, architect of nineteenth-century education in India, 'jewel in the imperial crown', had inspired generations of young imperialists with his *Lays of Ancient Rome*. The example of the one empire sanctioned its successor, which reached its zenith in 1897, when, in the words of its most eloquent chronicler, James Morris,

> the British had chosen to commemorate [Queen Victoria's] Diamond Jubilee as a festival of Empire. They were in possession that day of the largest Empire ever known to history, and since a large part of it had been acquired during the sixty years of Victoria's reign, it seemed proper to honour the one with the other. It would mark this moment of British history as an Imperial moment, a Roman moment. It would proclaim to the world, flamboyantly, that England was far more than England: that beneath the Queen's dominion lay a quarter of the earth's land surface, and nearly a quarter of its people – literally, as Christopher North the poet had long before declared it, an Empire on which the sun never set.

Only two years later, the reverses of the Boer War indicated that the imperial sun was '*now . . . less powerful*'. It declined further during the Great War which, on the analogy of the wars of ancient Greece and ancient Rome, at first seemed to offer the educated legionaries of a later empire the prospect of a place in both history and literature. In the poems of 1914 and the first half of 1915, there are countless references to sword and legion, but almost none to gun and platoon. In 1916, Siegfried Sassoon could still write 'We are the happy legion'. Our neighbour, Edmund Blunden, carried a copy of Caesar's *De Bello Gallico* in his pack through some of the worst fighting of the war and, when it was over, sat down to write a *De Bello Germanico* of his own. In the 1940s, another generation of reinforcements for the frontiers of empire trudged through such of Caesar's campaigns as that in Aquitania:

> The battle was long and fierce. The Satiates, with the confidence of previous victories, felt that upon their own courage depended the safety of all Aquitania: the Romans were eager to have it seen what they could accomplish under a young leader without the commander-in-chief and the rest of the legions. At last, however, after heavy casualties the enemy fled from the field. A large number of them were slain; and then Crassus turned direct from his march and began to attack the stronghold of the Satiates. When they offered a brave resistance he brought up mantlets and towers. The enemy at one time attempted a sortie, at another pushed mines as far as the ramp and the mantlets – and in mining the Aquitani are by far the most experienced of men, because in many localities among them there are copper-mines and diggings. When they perceived that by reason of the efficiency of our troops no advantage was to be gained by these expedients, they sent deputies to Crassus and besought him to accept their surrender.
>
> Their request was granted, and they proceeded to deliver up their arms as ordered.

Those who chose *The Gallic War* as a staple text for schoolboys' consumption intended them to learn from its example; to become as eager, indefatigable, implacable, resourceful, and (finally) merciful in defending and extending the British Empire as was Crassus in defending and extending the Roman.

Looking back through a post-colonial telescope, it is surprising to see how determined were the descendants of colonized Britons to remember only the commendable achievements of the conquerors and colonizers: their laws, their mosaics, their roads. The reason, of course, was that those achievements of the Roman Empire were held to justify our own. I heard only one dissonant voice, that of a poet, William Cowper, whose 'Boadicea' was to be found in *The Dragon Book of Verse*:

When the British warrior queen,
  Bleeding from the Roman rods,
Sought, with an indignant mien,
  Counsel of her country's gods,

Sage beneath a spreading oak
  Sat the Druid, hoary chief;
Ev'ry burning word he spoke
  Full of rage and full of grief.

'Princess! if our aged eyes
  Weep upon thy matchless wrongs,
'Tis because resentment ties
  All the terrors of our tongues.

Rome shall perish – write that word
  In the blood that she has spilt;
Perish, hopeless and abhorr'd,
  Deep in ruin as in guilt.

Rome, for empire far renown'd,
  Tramples on a thousand states;
Soon her pride shall kiss the ground –
  Hark! the Gaul is at her gates.

Other Romans shall arise,
  Heedless of a soldier's name;
Sounds, not arms, shall win the prize,
  Harmony the path to fame.

Then the progeny that springs
   From the forests of our land,
Arm'd with thunder, clad with wings,
   Shall a wider world command.

Regions Caesar never knew,
   Thy posterity shall sway,
Where his eagles never flew,
   None invincible as they.'

Such the bard's prophetic words,
   Pregnant with celestial fire,
Bending, as he swept the chords
   Of his sweet but awful lyre.

She, with all a monarch's pride,
   Felt them in her bosom glow;
Rush'd to battle, fought, and died;
   Dying, hurl'd them at the foe.

'Ruffians, pitiless as proud,
   Heav'n awards the vengeance due;
Empire is on us bestow'd,
   Shame and ruin wait for you.'

I don't think this poem was discussed in class, because for years I
thought it a prophecy of the greater empire that would succeed
the Roman; only later seeing that, if 'sounds, not arms, shall win
the prize', the bard must have been prophesying the rise of a language and literature that would replace Latin. I suspect, however,
that Cowper meant us to recognize that Boadicea did not fully
understand 'the bard's prophetic words'.

   This was the first of many battle poems in *The Dragon Book of
Verse*, an anthology specially prepared for the school by one of
its English masters, W.A.C. Wilkinson, and his brother, N.H.W.
Published by the Clarendon Press in 1935, *The Dragon Book*
carried the name of the school – as the *Oxford Books* it so resem-
bled (gold lettering on a blue buckram spine) carried the name

HENRY V AT THE SIEGE OF HARFLEUR

ONCE more unto the breach, dear friends, once more;
Or close the wall up with our English dead!

From *The Dragon Book of Verse*

of the university – to 'the round earth's imagined corners'. Like them, it is a period-piece revealing of British middle-class attitudes between the wars. Warfare is a major theme: from Byron's 'The Destruction of Sennacherib' and his Waterloo stanzas from *Childe Harold's Pilgrimage* to poems of the Great War by Laurence Binyon, Rupert Brooke, Julian Grenfell, and Charles Hamilton Sorley. In between Sennacherib and the Somme, we followed the Roman eagles to the Battle of Lake Regillus, and a variety of flags and banners to Agincourt, Harfleur, Bannockburn, Corunna, Hohenlinden, Naseby; and we shipped with

Hereward the Wake, Don John of Austria on a 'slaughter-painted poop', and Sir Richard Grenville aboard the *Revenge*. Responding, no doubt, to the preferences of the *Blue Dragon's* more peaceable Skipper, many great sea poems were there: 'The Ballad of Sir Patrick Spens', songs from *The Tempest*, Coleridge's 'Rime of the Ancient Mariner', Campbell's 'Ye Mariners of England', Flecker's 'The Old Ships', Masefield's 'Cargoes' and 'Sea Fever'.

A result of the imperial aspirations underlying – and sometimes overlying – such poems was the torrent of magical place-names that poured from our blue cornucopia: Cape St Vincent, Cathay, Damascus, Desenzano, Marathon, Nineveh, Ophir, Samarkand, Tusculum, and Tartary. They sparkled on the page and reverberated in the head quite unlike the names encountered in Geography lessons.

Despite the plenitude of ancient names, a fair number of modern poets were represented in the book (if only one was a woman and three were American), but so far as subject matter was concerned, the Middle Ages eclipsed the Modern. We met 'The Lady of Shalott', 'La Belle Dame Sans Merci', Tennyson's King Arthur, Spenser's Red-Cross Knight, and Robin Hood in a couple of ballads. We met them in a rural England with only one city: the London of Wordsworth's sonnet 'Composed upon Westminster Bridge', Bridges' 'London Snow', and Johnson's 'By the Statue of King Charles at Charing Cross'.

It is easy to deplore the male and martial bias of *The Dragon Book of Verse*, but it needs to be seen in its historical context, and what other school ever cared enough for poetry to commission its own anthology? No book I have ever owned has given me more pleasure or, I believe, more profit.

At the eleventh hour of the eleventh day of the eleventh month of 1942, past and present came together at a tall stone cross, overlooking the River Cherwell, incised with the names of eighty-three boys and masters killed in the War to end Wars, those followed by the Latin coda: 'NOMEN EORUM VIVIT IN

SAECULA SAECULORUM'. Two hundred and fifty service sheets fluttered in the wind as we sang the hymn beginning

> O valiant hearts, who to your glory came
> Through dust of conflict and through battle flame . . .

A boy read the lines from Binyon's poem 'For the Fallen':

> They shall grow not old, as we that are left grow old:
> Age shall not weary them, nor the years condemn.
> At the going down of the sun and in the morning
> We will remember them.

And we responded, as instructed by the service sheet, 'We will remember them.'

Hum then (looking like Cowper's 'Druid, hoary chief') spoke of the Old Dragons killed since the last Armistice Day service. One was a sailor, lost on his first voyage, and there were three fighter-pilots, two of them shot down in the Malta convoy action on the 12th of August. At the end of the service, two Army buglers sounded the 'Last Post' and 'Reveille', and we straggled back to our classrooms blowing into our cold hands.

When he was speaking of the dead fighter-pilots, I think Hum quoted from John Pudney's poem 'For Johnny':

> Do not despair
> For Johnny-head-in-air;
> He sleeps as sound
> As Johnny underground.

> Fetch out no shroud
> For Johnny-in-the-cloud;
> And keep your tears
> For him in after years.

> Better by far
> For Johnny-the-bright-star,
> To keep your head,
> And see his children fed.

This and the poem that prompted it – Heinrich Hoffmann's 'Story of Johnny Head-in-Air' (found in *The Golden Staircase*, Part 2) – prompted my own first attempt at poetry. Hearing on the news of air battles over the Pacific between American Mustang fighters and Japanese Zeros, I wrote an execrable ballad about a fighter-pilot (also called Johnny), who 'got a Zero'. Merciful oblivion has closed over my 'hero' as completely as the ocean over his victim, and no doubt I would have forgotten the occasion altogether but for the instant knowledge it brought: that what I most wanted to do in the world was to write poems.

The term that had begun with 'Onward Christian Soldiers' ended – as would subsequent terms – with a thunderous rendering of the school song, the 'Carmen Draconiense'. I don't think I was ever deluded into thinking this poetry, but one stanza used to touch me obscurely:

> There are Dragons in lands far apart,
> Where July is as cold as December;
> But within they've a warmth at the heart,
> And a something that makes them remember!
> So they think of the days of their youth,
> And they drain to the dregs of the flagon
> To the school-house afar, on the banks of the Cher,
> And the health of the conquering Dragon!

I pictured myself beside my New Zealand cousin Ray, then on the ice-encrusted bridge of a destroyer shepherding a convoy to Murmansk.

Christmas brought fantasies ancient as well as modern: Dinky Toy models of a Spitfire and a Hurricane, Charlotte M. Yonge's novel *The Little Duke*, and Kipling's *Puck of Pook's Hill* (the school's 'Holiday Reading'). I responded particularly to Kipling's propagandist lesson in living history, identifying myself with the boy Dan who, having 'come to grief over his Latin', was transported by a memory of Macaulay's *Lays of Ancient Rome* into the life of Roman legionaries on Hadrian's Wall, defending that frontier of their empire against the barbarians. Most of all I liked Kipling's 'Song to Mithras', a poem already encountered in *The Dragon Book of Verse*:

> Mithras, God of the Morning, our trumpets waken the Wall!
> 'Rome is above the Nations, but Thou art over all!'
> Now as the names are answered, and the guards are marched away,
> Mithras, also a soldier, give us strength for the day!

Invoked in subsequent stanzas as 'God of the Noontide', 'God of the Sunset', and 'God of the Midnight', he was finally urged: 'Mithras, also a soldier, teach us to die aright!' Only later did it strike me how many poems in our anthology offered lessons in dying.

★

In 1943, I felt the first slow movement of the merry-go-round of the seasons. Spring was a damp sandpit, where we strafed each other's Dinky Toy tanks and troop-carriers; summer, the season of marbles – clouded aggies, spirals filled with a frozen flame – chasing each other across the playground; autumn, the time of conkers, toughened in the oven, threaded on a bootlace for single combat, to conquer or be conquered; winter, best of all, the rugger season, smelling of new grass and new boot-leather softened with dubbin.

That summer, we explored the north bank of the Cherwell, or as much of it as lay within the school grounds, always returning to the Dragon Barge. This was not a barge at all, but a ship-like structure on the bank with a magnificent dragon figurehead, a high pointed stern, and a long deck in between. From either end, it looked like a beached and dismasted clipper. Only from the south could one see what it was: a changing room for the relays of would-be swimmers, each harnessed to a long pole in the hands of a master who strolled up and down the jetty shouting encouragement: 'Kick like a frog. That's better!'

The Barge

Awaiting our turn, we tried to catch the spoked thistledown freewheeling on the wind, or a sculling water-boatman, or watched the punts poled past by elegant undergraduates.

As our reading extended, the placid Cherwell became, in turn, the Iser rolling rapidly, Father Tiber, the great grey-green greasy Limpopo, and each of the seven seas. A high proportion of our favourite books involved shipwrecks on islands – the war heightening our awareness of both – and the adventures of Jim Hawkins and Long John Silver, Robinson Crusoe and Masterman Ready, inspired the boardings and sinkings, the marlin-spiking mutinies we survived on the pitching deck of the Dragon Barge.

That autumn, the Cherwell became another, more majestic, river – 'and the fog rose out of the Oxus stream' – with the arrival at the school of a small boy with a large name, Richard Rustom Kharsedji Sorabji. He was too honest to claim direct descent from the heroes of Arnold's 'Sohrab and Rustum' (who clashed so resoundingly in *The Dragon Book of Verse*), but at the

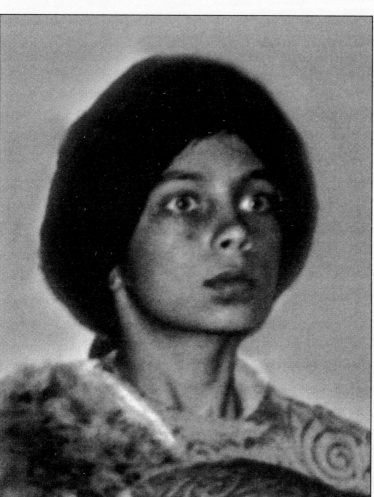

Richard Rustom Kharsedji Sorabji

same time too intelligent to disclaim a connection with them. He came, therefore, trailing clouds of glory, his conversation iridescent with jewelled turbans, scimitars and silken cushions. He introduced us to a subcontinent never conquered by the Romans, and to regiments with resonant names – Bengal Lancers, Gurkhas, and Rajputs – now fighting for the King-

Emperor of our coins. It would be some years before I would presume to call myself a friend of this exotic Maharajahling, but from the start I think I sensed a common bond: we were both foreigners, who could say (as our teachers would remind us): '*civis Romanus sum*'. We were proud of the lands of our fathers – though I might have admitted to myself that the Moguls were grander than the Maoris – but no less proud to be British.

All this romance was not only in our heads. It was also under our hands: in the school museum, a chamber of horrors and marvels above the carpentry workshop in the centre of the playground. Taken there in a Latin class to see the Roman coins, glass phials, hypocaust tiles, and surgical instruments (my father was impressed by those), we returned on our own to glut our curiosity. Everything in the museum had been given by someone, and I would wonder how one came to own – or could give away – an elephant's foot, the man-trap jaws of a shark, a stuffed golden eagle, or a woman's bracelet cut from the stomach of an Indian crocodile. For the naturalist, there were drawers of birds' eggs and butterflies: for the historian, lamps from a pharaoh's tomb, Stone Age arrowheads, an Anglo-Saxon comb, assegais from Africa, bayonets from the Somme.

There was something for everyone in the museum, and that was emblematic of the ethos of the school. The Skipper had believed – and his apostles upheld his belief – that every child should be interested in *something*. Their task was to identify that something and develop the interest in it. The something might be spiders or spin-bowling or poetry. I never heard it suggested that spiders or spin-bowling were more (or less) important than poetry. If something was important to *you*, that was enough: you would be guided to books on your topic in the library: the spider-boy would be sent to study the bottled horrors in the University Museum; the bowling fanatic would be told to watch the wrist action of first-class cricketers at net practice in the University Parks; and it was suggested that I should start my own poetry anthology.

The Museum

I therefore bought a hard-backed notebook and wrote on the inside cover: 'Poem Book/Collected by J. Stallworthy/Index at back of book'. I never got around to preparing the index, but did cut out fifty-four lyric poems – I don't like to think from what butchered books – and stuck them in. A high proportion were Nature poems, some by good poets, others by unheard-of poets of whom one would not wish to hear more. Two – but only two – of my choices also appeared in *The Dragon Book of Verse*: Sir Walter Scott's 'Hunting Song' and Browning's 'Pippa Passes'. I wish I could claim that my 'Poem Book' shows precocious literary judgement. I cannot, but I think it shows imagination on the part of whoever proposed it. He or she could have been any one of a dozen people.

Who were they, these paragons? They were not paragons, they were enthusiasts, celebrants of the good life (in some cases, I suspect, because the Great War had left them grateful to be alive). 'Fuzz' had been wounded in France and lacked an eye in a badly scarred face. 'Tubby' was said to have a silver plate in his head, which explained and excused his occasional rages. When the spittle began to fly, we knew what would follow – chalk bullets, the board-rubber, a book or two – and, in the trenches, we gripped the lids of our desks ready to jerk them up when a projectile came our way. One day, a Canadian Army driver parked under Tubby's classroom window and, after listening for some minutes, said it was the nearest he had been to the war so far.

Then there was S.P.B. Mais. He was not on the permanent staff, but came in on Saturday mornings to talk to one of the top English sets. The door would fly open and in he would bustle (greatcoated and mufflered on even the brightest day), talking volubly about Alexander Pope or Lord Byron as though they were personal friends. A racy portrait of the life would be followed by an account of the poems – how and for whom they were written, how they worked. They worked because their words worked, each pulling its weight in the line. He spoke, as a professional writer, of other professional writers:

'Listen for the assonance . . . notice the placing of the caesura . . . how the enjambement speeds up the line.'

Propelled up and down the aisles of the class by an apparent internal combustion engine, fuelled with enthusiasm, he would start to sweat. Off would come the greatcoat, the muffler, a checked tweed jacket, a pullover, a sleeveless pullover. Only the school bell, it seemed, saved him from indecent exposure.

For 'prep', his class and others would be required to write a passage of blank verse in the style of Cowper's 'The Task' or in the alliterative line of 'Beowulf', or couplets in the manner of Pope's 'Rape of the Lock'. The best of these (never mine) would be printed in *The Draconian*, the school magazine. I delighted in such ventriloquial exercises, and learnt from them more about how poets and poems worked than ever I did in those years from conventional literary study.

★

The laws of the Dragon School were Roman, well-codified, firm but fair – as I learnt on the occasion when I took the law into my own right hand.

I was in Mr Retey's French class. He didn't like me, nor I him. Whenever there was an exercise to be handed back, the mistakes singled out for sarcastic mockery were invariably mine. I bore this with a fixed smile for the better part of a term, until one day everything changed. A lesson was rising to the usual climax – he cataloguing the imbecilities of *ce pauvre idiot*, me grinning like an Aztec skull – but then, instead of laying the contemptible exercise on my desk, he spun it with a deft back-hand into my face. The touch of the paper triggered a Pacific volcano. Subterranean pressure lifted me to my feet, retracted my right arm, and drove its fist into his face. He crashed backwards, spreadeagled against his desk: for me, a moment of sheer exhilaration succeeded by a moment of sheer terror. Something (not lava) was running down my leg as I moved swiftly towards the door. A seventh sense told me he was in pursuit and about to deliver a mighty kick. Thanks to my father's rugger coaching, I side-stepped and had the satisfaction of hearing shoe-leather strike wood as I reached the door and wriggled through. The door slammed, and in the terrible silence that followed, I made a decision: I would beard the Dragon in his den.

The headmaster's study was some distance away, in the dark depths of the School House. It had been pointed out to me, though I had never been inside. I knocked on the door with tender knuckles.

'Come in.' I went into the smoky cavern. The Dragon was at his desk, writing. Slowly Joc turned his saurian head and, looking at me over his spectacles, said out of the side of his mouth furthest from his cigarette:

'Shouldn't you be in French?'

'Yes.'

'Then why aren't you?'

'Please, sir, I punched Mr Retey.'

'How hard did you punch Mr Retey?'

Joc: the Dragon in his den

'Not as hard as I wanted.'

'I see. And why did you punch Mr Retey?' I told him, and he said I could go. Only when I was out in the corridor did it strike me that at no time had he taken the cigarette from his mouth and, when I left, its ash was an inch long.

My parents, when I confessed that evening, were dismayed.

My father knew I would be expelled (he told my mother who told *me* after the verdict had been announced), but didn't share that knowledge with me. Perhaps remembering his own near-expulsion from Otago, he let me know I had his rueful support, and nothing more was said about my action or its consequences during the dismal week that followed. Another week was well advanced when I was called back to the Dragon's den and knocked on the door, expecting this time to be eaten alive.

'I've spoken to some of the boys in your class', he said, 'and to Mr Retey, and it's clear to me that you both deserve six of the best. However, small boys can't go round punching large masters, so you'd better go and apologize to him.'

I said nothing, waiting for the ultimate sentence.

'That's all,' he barked, and I bolted into the warm sun.

I remembered that day some years later, when I learned that Dragon justice could also be draconian and fair.

It wasn't that I didn't like Mr Martin or had reason to suppose he didn't like me, but I thought he was 'fleb' (Dragon-speak for 'feeble') and devised a booby-trap for him. Half a dozen cardboard 'detonators', taken from Christmas crackers, were pinned to the top of the classroom door and the lintel above it minutes before a lesson was due to begin.

We heard his step outside, the door-handle turned, and the detonators went off like rifle fire above his head. He fell into the room, writhing and sobbing on the floor. Somebody ran for the school nurse, and in half an hour I was again in the Dragon's den. Joc was tapping his leg with a four-foot cane.

'You've taken unfair advantage', he said, 'of a young and vulnerable master still suffering from his experiences in the war' – I had never heard of shell-shock – 'and I am going to beat you very hard indeed.' He did, and as the captain of the school rugger XV slowly straightened up, he said:

'That's that. Are you going to win on Saturday?'

★

By the spring of 1944, the tide of the war had turned, bringing the Pied Piper's children back across the Atlantic: among them, my first friend, Roger Norrington. His career as a conductor had started at the Wayside Nursery School, but not as it was to continue. Climbing on to a chair to conduct the percussion group, he fell backwards and hit his head so hard that a new conductor had to be found. He cared about music as I about poetry, and soon after his arrival at the Dragon was coaxing tunes from his violin while, in the music hut next door, mine was articulating my teacher's anguish. The Norringtons lived opposite Woodstock Close and, after school and at weekends, Roger and I would play together until, in the spring of 1945, we moved.

I knew that change was in the air when my father drove us out of Oxford to see a large dark house on Shotover, one of the three hills overlooking Oxford.

'Too big,' said my mother.

'Too expensive,' said my father, and drove us home.

Some weeks later, he said: 'I see "Shotover Edge" is still on the market and its price has come down. Let's have another look at it.' On this visit, he discovered why its price had come down: the house drew its water from a well and this had failed – the result, it was said, of tank manoeuvres on the hill cracking the rock strata.

'What about water from the mains?'

'It can't be pumped so high.'

This was just the sort of problem he liked. The house became his patient and, in a couple of days, he had worked out an operation that would cure it. He went to see the widow who owned 'Shotover Edge'.

'The house is too high for water from the mains, but the bottom of the garden isn't. You could pipe mains water that far and then use the pump from the dry well to pump it up to the house.'

'Don't you want to buy it?'

'Yes, but I can't afford the price you can ask for it now.'

Shotover Edge

'You've solved the problem,' she said. 'I should like you to have it for the price I'm asking now.'

And so we moved.

*

It was a large house with a large terraced garden, and I think our happiness in both over subsequent decades owed something to the national rejoicing as we moved in. VE Day brought church bells and bonfires, few more splendid than that in the Dragon School playground (kindled only after the surrounding buildings had been hosed with a stirrup-pump). At its top was a gas-mask, at its base many thunder-flashes, and the science master persuaded its flames to burn first red, then green. From Shotover that night, we could see a constellation of other fires on the invisible hills round Oxford.

I think my father chose our house because its trees reminded him of New Zealand. The only picture he had brought from what would always be for him 'the great good place' was a sombre oil, by C. Bloomfield, of the New Zealand 'bush' with larches and kauris. As a Boy Scout, he had taken part in the ceremonial hand-over to the nation of one of the few surviving stands of those 100-foot native giants. 'Shotover Edge' had no kauris, but a great many larches, and as my mother set about making curtains for the house, my father and I spent happy weekends as tree-surgeons.

Any diseased or badly damaged tree had to come down, and there was an antipodean ritual for this. He would decide where it was to fall and mark the line with his handkerchief. If other trees were at risk, I would climb the doomed trunk with a hand-saw and lop off the branches that threatened them. Next, his axe would make the white chips fly, cutting out a broad wedge facing our marker. Then together at the two ends of the six-foot cross-cut saw we would deliver the *coup de grâce*. There was an art to this and we were artists, drawing the blade straight in a steady rhythm until it sang its plangent elegy for the tree. When the tree groaned, we withdrew the blade and watched our saw-cut open and the axe-cut close as the trunk fell forward (usually) on to the handkerchief. Finally, while I axed off the remaining branches, he would clean, sharpen, and oil the cross-cut before buttoning it up in its canvas and leather case.

'A good workman', he said, 'looks after his tools. You can sharpen and oil the axe.'

The same precept was to be applied in another area of an Anglo-New Zealander's education: rugger boots had to be cleaned and oiled after matches. By 1946, my father's coaching was showing results and I was playing right-wing in the school's first XV. I was small and not particularly fast, but obedient to his shouts from the touch-line – '*Run*. For God's sake *RUN!*' – I scored a few tries. After the best of these, the referee announced: 'Try awarded to the House of Stallworthy!' Father and son were never united in a moment of purer pleasure.

Perhaps to complement or counterbalance all the nautical

Youth at the helm

novels I was reading, or perhaps to replicate another of my father's antipodean pleasures, I was 'indentured' to a school master who skippered a training-yacht on the Norfolk Broads. In the course of three week-long voyages, I and five other Ordinary Boys graduated to Able Boy, Leading Boy, and Boatswain in a series of tests, the last of them involving command of the ship and her crew for twenty-four hours.

A salutary counterbalance to this physical education was provided by my burgeoning friendship with Richard Sorabji, the shades of whose ancestors were not to be propitiated with axes, rugger balls, and running bowlines. He lived a couple of miles away, and almost every evening, in term and out, would cycle up to Shotover after supper and we would go for a walk and talk of setting the Cherwell on fire. Richard was a classicist – soon to be a classical scholar (as I was not or ever would be) – with a love of country churches. Did he, on one of our nocturnal walks, tell me of the new book by another lover of country churches, or did I read in *The Draconian*, under the heading 'O.D. Publications', the review of *New Bats in Old Belfries*, by 'John Betjeman (1920)'? Probably both. The reviewer, S.P.B. Mais, wrote:

Memorableness is one of the prime necessities of poetry, and I for one shall never again cycle Dragon-wards without shouting to the over-taking bus drivers –

> *'Belbroughton Road is bonny, and pinkly bursts the spray*
> *Of prunus and forsythia across the public way.'*

Or –

> *'And a constant sound of flushing runneth from windows where*
> *The toothbrush too is airing in this new North Oxford air*
> *From Summerfields to Lynams, the thirsty tarmac dries,*
> *And a Cherwell mist dissolveth on elm-discovering skies.'*

Betjeman's strength lies, as a poet's strength should, in original, surprising, even at times Homeric, epithets.

How apt and, once read, how inevitable are the *'redden'd remorselessness'* of Cardigan Street, the *'hassocky'* smell of churches, the *'Eighteen-sixty'* Early English, the *'beefy'* A.T.S.* *'without their hats,'*

---

* Members of the Auxiliary Territorial Service for women (1938–48).

the bedroom windows of St. Enodoc on Sunday afternoon where '*double-aspirined*' a mother sleeps, the '*whacking great*' sunsets of Lincolnshire, the '*polychromatical*' lacing of St. Barnabas's bricks, the '*Blunden*' time of wild flowers, the '*amber-dyed*' mud of the sunlit Thames, and, to be serious for a moment, the '*hollow unhallowed*' VE day . . .

If I could afford it, I would distribute free copies of this admirable slim volume among all schools to give boys and girls a model to copy. He is an ideal poet for adolescents to try their teeth on.

I was given a copy of 'this admirable slim volume' (the first I possessed by a living poet other than A.A. Milne) and found not only a Dragon poet, but a poet of the Here and Now, *my* Here and Now, who wrote of 'Lynams' and 'Summerfields' (a prep-school down the road, which we always beat at rugger). Many Remembrance Day services had given me a feel for the emotion behind Betjeman's elegy, 'In Memory of Basil, Marquess of Dufferin and Ava' – though my beginner's Greek was insufficient for me to spot his hexameters:

> Friend of my youth, you are dead!
>   and the long peal pours from the steeple
> Over this sunlit quad
>   in our University city
> And soaks in Headington stone.
>   Motionless stand the pinnacles.
> Under a flying sky
>   as though they too listened and waited
> Like me for your dear return
>   with a Bullingdon noise of an evening
> In a Sports-Bugatti from Thame
>   that belonged to a man in Magdalen.
> Friend of my youth, you are dead!
>   and the quads are empty without you.
>
> Then there were people about.
>   Each hour, like an Oxford archway,

Opened on long green lawns
 and distant unvisited buildings
And you my friend were explorer
 and so you remained to me always
Humorous, reckless, loyal –
 my kind, heavy-lidded companion.
Stop, oh many bells, stop
 pouring on roses and creeper
Your unremembering peal
 this hollow, unhallowed V.E. day, –
I am deaf to your notes and dead
 by a soldier's body in Burma.

The poem that took me by the throat, however, and caused a constriction in the chest, was 'A Subaltern's Love-Song':

Miss J. Hunter Dunn, Miss J. Hunter Dunn,
Furnish'd and burnish'd by Aldershot sun,
What strenuous singles we played after tea,
We in the tournament – you against me!

Love-thirty, love-forty, oh! weakness of joy,
The speed of a swallow, the grace of a boy,
With carefullest carelessness, gaily you won,
I am weak from your loveliness, Joan Hunter Dunn.

I can't claim that my physical response to this was simply a precocious critical recognition of the best poem in the book. The truth is both more bizarre and more mundane: for a year I had been under the spell of a rare creature, a female Dragon, called *Edith* Dunn. There were few girls at the school. They were admitted only if they had male Dragons in the family; were prepared to accept the school discipline, and take part in its organized games. Like every calf in love, I told myself my favourite was 'unlike the others' – Helen, who sold kisses for sixpence in the Dragon Lane, or Sonia, who was beaten for carving her name on her desk. Edith was my *princesse lointaine* and 'she

The Dragon rugger XV with the RNC Dartmouth Drakes

walked unaware of her own increasing beauty'. We had shared
the Lower 2 prize for Latin. No doubt I was struggling to keep
up with her, to be noticed: forever without success, for she left
the following summer.

★

Joc Lynam had been at Rugby and, one day, leaving the field
with my father after a rugger match, persuaded him (probably
no difficult matter) that he 'should put me down' for the same
school. To prepare me for leaving home, it was agreed that I
should board for my last year at the Dragon, so in September
1947 I moved my trunk and tuckbox into the School House.

Never was a schoolboy less homesick. I was captain of the
rugger XV and, auditioned for a part in the Christmas production of Gilbert and Sullivan's *Patience*, was enlisted as a Heavy
Dragoon. Even had I been able to sing like Roger Norrington
– star of the previous year's *Iolanthe* – I would have preferred to
be a Heavy Dragoon than Bunthorn (a Fleshly Poet) or
Grosvenor (an Idyllic Poet). I knew I wanted to be a poet: what
kind of poet I didn't know, but it wasn't Fleshly or Idyllic.

Patience was produced by the chief English master, a ginger-haired dynamo called 'Bruno' Brown, who had been producing Gilbert and Sullivan operas at the school for the past twenty-six years. In action – and between late September and mid-November he was never out of action – he was like an Indian deity with many hands: one flourishing a conductor's baton, one turning the pages of a score, one sketching the scene-painter's canvas, one beating his forehead in exasperation. He plotted in advance every movement and gesture, every piece of 'stage business', every entrance and exit, even every inflection of the voice. *Patience* was his favourite Gilbert and Sullivan opera, and with his white wand he turned shy boys into posturing Poets, ragged instrumentalists into a harmonious orchestra.

For the least musical of his Dragons – one forbidden to sing two difficult choruses – the rewards of those eight weeks were both social and professional: the pleasure of being part of a greater whole (as in a rugger team), and the pleasures of the text. Those last were very similar to the pleasures I had derived from Betjeman's poems: their presentation of the past as breathing present, their satire, their metrical and rhyming invention. The connection may not be fortuitous since, in Bruno's 1920 production of *The Pirates of Penzance*, his wand had turned Betjeman into a buxom Ruth. Gilbert and Sullivan may have helped turn him into a poet.

The following summer I returned to Bruno's stage, in doublet and hose, as Fabian in *Twelfth Night*. For this nonentity, the pleasures of the production were even greater than the Heavy Dragoon's. He had read several Shakespeare plays, learnt dozens of his speeches, and seen the film of Olivier's *Henry V* (four times), but had never *lived* one of the plays before. When it was over, Bruno asked the members of his English set to write a sixth Act of *Twelfth Night*. My 'Malvolio's Revenge' was unlike Shakespeare's five in a number of respects: one being that two speeches contained sonnets. I had read a number of Shakespeare's sonnets in *The Dragon Book of Verse* and thought that, like his speeches in the anthology, they were taken from his plays. No one pointed out my mistake.

★

At our last Assembly, with breaking voices, we sang:

> Time, like an ever-rolling stream,
> Bears all its sons away . . .

and then, once more with feeling, the 'Carmen Draconiense'. From the Old Hall, Leavers who were boarders (a category that, significantly, did not include girls) strode, with the studied gravity of young South Sea Islanders heading for the Sacred Grove where boys became men, to their own rite of passage: The Sex Talk. This was traditionally held in Hum's sitting-room (perhaps to underscore the imminence of adulthood). We filed in with our eyes on the floor, lest they reveal our curiosity and unease: most of us then – even the obstetrician's son – knew little or nothing about sex.

When we were disposed among the cushions, the old chief rose to his feet. He was wearing a pale grey suit which, with his white hair and white moustache, gave him a blanched look that the pink rose in his buttonhole served to emphasize rather than relieve. He blew his nose on a white handkerchief, then cleared his throat and, as he began to speak, I realized he was nervous. He would have preferred to be talking to us about poetry, and his approach to his subject was as much poetical-pastoral as biological:

'You will have seen a bee with pollen on its proboscis enter a flower to sip its nectar and, at the same time, fertilize it.' (I had not and, indeed, had never had a biology lesson.) 'Well, it's the same with a man and a woman. After marriage, a man will put his proboscis – his penis – into his wife's flower – her vagina – and fertilize her with his seed . . .'

Hum

As he mumbled on, I found myself staring at the rose in his buttonhole, and a memory of Ariel's song, from *The Dragon Book of Verse*, came unhelpfully to mind:

> Where the bee sucks, there suck I:
> In a cowslip's bell I lie . . .

Hum and Mrs Hum: no, it was not possible. A wild hilarity surged through me. I dared not catch another initiate's eye, but could feel the sofa shaking.

Perhaps Hum thought we were wriggling with embarrassment or 'wanting to be excused' and, mercifully, he let us go. We fled to the cricket pavilion, laughing hysterically and choking on regurgitated gobbets of pastoral biology.

There were few straight faces at the Leavers' Lunch, and never did we go in a higher good humour to the grand finale of a Dragon School summer term: the Rag Regatta. By tradition, this was a combination of aquatic tournament and pantomime. Boys, standing in canoes, jousted with mops; then a puntful of paddling Maoris, extravagantly tattooed with blue Cherwell mud, raced a similar war canoe of painted Picts.

The Draconian reported the climactic imperial pantomime in unselfconsciously racist detail:

In one slight pause, Hitler drifted by lounging in a punt with an S.S. man in charge.

[Then] a warning was issued to any member of the staff thinking of joining Frank Cary's School in E. Africa as to what conditions he might possibly expect. The poor schoolmaster was faced with three coal-black pupils who arrived by canoe. They drank his ink, gobbled up his pencils, and made necklaces of his books. Just when he thought he had got them under control a nasty sort of ape appeared and caused havoc again. Then a very wild bushman came and threw a knife with deadly accuracy at his blackboard. Of course the poor man finished in the river, and the rest too for that matter: for as one small spectator put it, they were very 'dirty' men and badly needed a wash!

By evening I was home, myself washing off the last of my Maori tattoos from the bottom of the Cherwell's 'ever-rolling stream'.

4

Metrics

SOMEONE WHO KNEW I was going to Rugby – Bruno, perhaps, or S.P.B. Mais – had asked me if I had read Arnold's 'Rugby Chapel', which he said was 'a good poem prompted by a bad novel, *Tom Brown's Schooldays*'. The answer was no, I hadn't read either, but I would.

I was surprised to find the poem an elegy for Arnold's father, but liked it because, with the intense subjectivity of 13, I thought he sounded like *my* father:

> Cheerful, and helpful, and firm!
> . . .
> Languor is not in your heart,
> Weakness is not in your word,
> Weariness not on your brow.

If I was encouraged by 'Rugby Chapel', I was *dis*couraged by *Tom Brown's Schooldays*, although it began on familiar ground, the White Horse Hill, where we had picnic'd. The ground was also familiar in historical terms; the reader approaching Tom Brown's home by way of

> a magnificent Roman camp, and no mistake, with gates and ditch and mounds. . . . There is always a breeze in the 'camp' as it is called; and here it lies, just as the Romans left it, except that cairn on the

68

east side, left by Her Majesty's corps of Sappers and Miners the other day, when they and the Engineer officer had finished their sojourn there, and their surveys for the Ordnance Map of Berkshire. . . .

And now we leave the camp, and descend towards the west, and are on the Ash-down. We are treading on heroes. It is sacred ground for Englishmen, more sacred than all but one or two fields where their bones lie whitening. For this is the actual place where our Alfred won his great battle, the battle of Ashdown ('Æscendum' in the chroniclers), which broke the Danish power, and made England a Christian land.

This imperial overture announced the theme of the book and, it seemed, the principal activity of the school: fighting. 'From the cradle to the grave,' I was told, 'fighting, rightly understood, is the business, the real highest honestest business of every son of man.' Thomas Hughes introduced me to a new concept, 'manliness', and its much-used adjective 'manly', that gave off disturbing vibrations, though I was somewhat reassured that he spoke of 'Arnold's manly piety', and the poet's father, I gathered, didn't approve of fighting.

*

My own father valued the literal above the literary, but he had an intuitive sense of symbolism. On the morning of the day I was to go to Rugby, he said he had a job for me. Shouldering a spade and telling me to bring the wheelbarrow, which was full of earth and small saplings, he led me to the bottom of the garden.

'Those are chestnuts,' he said. 'I want you to plant them in a row.' So I dug a dozen holes, spread out a dozen lacy root-systems, shovelled in the earth, and stamped it down.

'By the time you leave Rugby', he said, 'they'll be as tall as you are, and when you're my age, they'll be shading the lawn.'

After lunch, I loaded my trunk and tuck-box into the boot of the car, and an hour later we swept into Rugby at twice the speed

– but with none of the drama – of the stage-coach that had delivered Tom Brown. Since I didn't have to present myself at Troy House until late afternoon and didn't want to say goodbye any sooner than I had to, I suggested we have a look at the Chapel. My parents agreed and we walked to the Close. It was exactly as Arnold had described it:

> The field
> Strewn with its dank yellow drifts
> Of withered leaves, and the elms,
> Fade into dimness apace,
> Silent; hardly a shout
> From a few boys late at their play!

Suddenly my father stopped and said: 'Look at this!' And in solemn chorus, two and half New Zealanders read out the inscription on the pink granite plaque in the red brick wall:

THIS STONE
COMMEMORATES THE EXPLOIT OF
WILLIAM WEBB ELLIS
WHO WITH A FINE DISREGARD FOR THE RULES OF FOOTBALL
AS PLAYED IN HIS TIME
FIRST TOOK THE BALL IN HIS ARMS AND RAN WITH IT
THUS ORIGINATING THE DISTINCTIVE FEATURE OF
THE RUGBY GAME
AD 1823

I was even more impressed to discover, in the Chapel, a marble memorial to Matthew Arnold flanked by matching memorials to two other nineteenth-century poets I had encountered in *The Dragon Book of Verse*: Walter Savage Landor and Arthur Hugh Clough. Each was commemorated by a quotation from one of his poems, and each quotation spoke of Death – as did another memorial on a nearby pillar. Under a carved relief copied from a photograph of the swan-necked Rupert Brooke – a photo-graph he captioned 'My Favourite Actress' – there was engraved the sonnet beginning 'If I should die'. I began to feel better about Rugby. At least, one would be in good company.

★

Rupert Brooke, 'My Favourite Actress'

Troy was an 'Overflow' House for new boys waiting for a place in one of the main Boarding Houses. I found the company there and in the high-ceilinged classrooms congenial enough, if less inspiring than that of the dead poets in Chapel. I was, however, thinking less about poetry than football that term.

Charlie Bagnall and I had played in the same Dragon School three-quarter line. Without his spectacles he seemed as blind as a bat, except on the rugger field where, directed by some batlike guidance system, he seldom missed a pass or a tackle. Finding ourselves now in the same House, we put our names down for the school's under-15 Young Guard trials, but were both too small and too slow. Bundled aside and relegated to the touchline, we spent our twilights together kicking a ball around a damp field, preparing for the day when we would be twice as large and twice as fast.

In the meantime, we were the proud 'fags' of an Old Dragon for whom that day had come. Peter Greenstreet was a scholar, in the Upper Bench (the top form), in the school's rugger XV and captain of its cricket XI. Four years before, the reviewer of a Dragon School *Henry IV, Part I*, had told readers of *The Draconian*: 'Greenstreet's Prince Hal was poised, clear-cut, easy and most attractive. . . . He gave us a madcap Prince to the life, and later he gave us the heroic Prince to the life.' Madame Cornuel claimed that 'No man is a hero to his valet', but that was how Peter Greenstreet seemed to his fags: a madcap in the House, heroic on the rugger field. Our duties were not demanding. We had to clean his shoes and his study every weekend, and we had to make him toast in front of an open fire at supper. He grumbled when Charlie Bagnall put boot-polish *inside* his shoes or I burnt his toast, but I don't remember him punishing us and I do remember him tipping us generously at the end of every term. We knew where his money came from and, indeed, played a small part in its acquisition. Every evening, Charlie and I took it in turns to go down town and buy him a 'green 'un' that gave the racing results. These might produce a whoop of delight or a groan of despair and, either way, we knew what would follow. He would take down from his bookcase one of a long line of notebooks (prominently marked ARISTOTLE or PLATO on the spine) and copy out the detail of the day's results into neat columns: race-track, 'going' (good to soft), horses, trainers, jockeys, odds. Next day, having studied the 'form' of the runners and checked the weather forecast, he would place his bets and win more often than he would lose. He had no private income, but the horses kept him in some style.*

Contrary to expectations engendered by *Tom Brown's Schooldays*, fags in Stanley House – where I went from Troy – received not only payment from their fag-masters, but also advice on what to read, how to improve their place-kicking or (of particular help to me) how to overcome fear of a tyrannical French master: 'Imagine him in the bath!' The sweetness and light, famously recommended by Matthew Arnold, were not, of course, everywhere on display in the House. There were rules and there were penalties for breaking them.

One evening in my first summer term I was late for bed, and the dormitory prefect offered me a choice of punishment: four strokes from his slipper or fourteen lines of verse – in twenty-four hours – on 'Procrastination is the thief of time'. Six months earlier I would have chosen the beating, as a form of central heating to which I was well accustomed, but it being a warm night and my nerve no longer in question, I chose the new challenge. Sleepy voices from shadowy beds fell silent one by one, but a voice in my head began repeating 'Procrastination is the thief of time' and then extending that sentence into other iambic

---

* Not true. Fifty years on, Peter Greenstreet says my memory deceives me: he 'was interested in horse-racing, yes', but has no recollection of sending us out for the racing papers or recording the results in notebooks; and, before the days of betting-shops, it would have been impossible for him to place bets. Ruefully, I must accept the dismaying fact that a memory I would have sworn to be true in a court of law is, at least in part, a case of False Memory Syndrome. Could both memories be at fault, at least in part? There seems no way of solving the mystery.

pentameter feet. I tapped them out with the fingers of my right
hand – one finger to one metrical foot – against my thigh (a
useful tactic that enabled one to compose poems in class with the
hand in one's pocket). In the small hours, crouching to make a
tent of my bedclothes and reaching for torch, envelope, and
pencil, I wrote:

> Procrastination is the thief of time,
> Who o'er the hedgerows of the sky doth race
> To strike betimes the clock-tower's mellow chime,
> And speed the hands around the patient face.
> With silent stride and hooded face he steals
> To where the bearded Time-God plies his scythe,
> And drawing close his dusky cowl, he kneels
> Behind a cloud bank, ere with movement lithe
> And serpentine he crawls to loose the bands
> That seal the hallowed sacks of time. Full then
> He fills his fists with the eternal sands,
> And with it dulls the eyes of idle men.
> Beware O mortal lest this fiend beguiles
> Your simple senses with his cunning wiles.

I thought a Shakespearean sonnet had to be written in
Shakespearean English, but the prefect said it would do, and the
following week I handed it in to my form-master as work allegedly prepared in a free prep.

My year as a boarder at the Dragon School had undoubtedly
eased the transition to Rugby, but it was a transition from tech-
nicolour to monochrome. The town was drab, the school more
formal, the teaching less dynamic, but with the onrush of
summer I began to feel more optimistic. Then came the note
from Arthur fforde, the 'Bodger', as the headmaster of Rugby
was traditionally called. I was summoned to his study in 'the
Barching Tower' (a corruption of Birching). I had never met him
and spent a worried hour or two with my friends rehearsing
crimes – real or conceivably attributable to me – that could have

come to his attention. Then the long walk to the scaffold, the stone steps, the door at which my knuckles for a moment mutinied. A voice said 'Come in' and 'Sit down' and 'How long have you been writing poems?' My form-master had given the Bodger my sonnet and he had underlined in red ink all the words with a long ī: *time, betimes, chime, silent stride.* . . .

'Did you know you were using so many?'

'No.'

'You've a good ear and you must learn to use it.' He told me about assonance (I wish he had also told me about poetic diction) and let me go.

I ran down the steps of the scaffold a reprieved man and stood on the ground a long moment with the sun on my face. The Bodger thought I could be a poet. I was on my way.

★

The way of an apprentice poet lies – like anyone else's – through acres of vegetable prose, but looking back I have more difficulty remembering the greens that sustained me through those years than the poppies or roses along the way. In morning chapel, there was the Bible on the back of its bronze eagle and the Psalter in our hands. The language of such books, flowing through one's head every schoolday for five years, leaves a rich deposit. I used to wish I could love God (mainly because it would have pleased my parents) as much as I loved the words and, even more, the cadences of His Book. It pleased me to meet them again in Bunyan's *Pilgrim's Progress* and in Milton's *Areopagitica*, as well as in his poems.

I remember reading *Gulliver's Travels* (the first three Parts only) and struggling with the concept of satire and how it differed from comedy. The difficulty, I now see, lay in understanding social satire when one didn't understand the ways of the society being satirized. The masters spoke of Indignation, but genuinely indignant satire – the fourth Part of *Gulliver's Travels*, *A Modest*

Proposal, and *Animal Farm* – we were left to discover on our own.
Discussed in class, they would have led to embarrassing questions
about our own lives and times that many masters (and, I suspect,
parents) wouldn't have welcomed. I particularly regret not
reading *A Modest Proposal* at school.* My view of empire would
have been different if I had.

If my recollections of prose texts read at Rugby are dim, this
must be, at least in part, because the teaching was dim. Mr
Gillon's class was a case in point. He told us:

'The only way to appreciate Shakespeare is to hear it, so
today we're going to read *Othello*. For the Moor we need a big
voice, a rich voice. Who's going to read the Moor? Well, perhaps
I should read the Moor.

'What about Iago? We want a tenor voice, a controlled,
cunning voice, with a good range. Bartlett? No, I don't think so.
I'd better read Iago.

'Desdemona now – one of the Bard's most attractive
women – young, trusting, tender. We need a light sweet voice.
Who'll read Desdemona? [*A fractional pause.*] No volunteers? All
right, I'll read Desdemona.'

He would then read them all – apart from a token Attendant
Lord or two – in the voice of the Conservative Party at
prayer.

Mr Tosswill was said to be different, for better and for worse:
dead keen on poetry (better), but the most feared disciplinarian
in the school (worse). Not that he ever beat anybody but, reput-
edly, his tongue could raise a weal that would outlast those of his
colleagues' sticks.

First impressions were unfavourable: far from looking as
striking as I thought someone dead keen on poetry should
look, he reminded me, in his black gown, of a closed umbrella

---

* Jonathan Swift, *A Modest Proposal for preventing the Children of Poor People
being a Burden to their Parents in the Country* (1729). Swift's savage satire proposed
that the children of the starving Irish could be sold as food for the rich in
England.

Mr Tosswill

or a hungry vulture. And like a vulture, he pounced on me at our first meeting in class. He asked a question, which I answered.

'What did you say?' Such was the menace in his voice that the room-temperature seemed to fall by twenty degrees.

Nervously, I repeated what I'd said.

'You forgot something!'

'What?'

'*What!* You forgot to say *Sir!* Come and see me at the end of the class!'

When I presented myself for sentencing, he gave me a lecture on Fundamental Courtesy and said: 'You will learn Keats's sonnet beginning "When I have fears that I may cease to be", so that his fear of death may instil a terror of Tosswill. Good morning.'

Learning the poem was no punishment. I'd long since discovered that, if I read a rhymed poem aloud to myself twice before going to bed, I would know it next morning. When I went to 'play it back' to Mr Tosswill (the *Mr* was apparently important), he asked me if I knew how old Keats was when he wrote it, and *why* he wrote it. I didn't. He said he was 22 and had a presentiment of early death from consumption, the disease that had killed his mother when he was 14. He died at 25. Did those facts, he asked, make me feel differently about the poem I had just learnt?

'Yes. . . . *Sir*,' I said.

'So they should, and never forget that Life is more important than Literature' (I could hear the capital Ls).

I remembered what he'd said when, in his next class, he made us read Keats's 'La Belle Dame Sans Merci'. Meeting this in *The Dragon Book of Verse*, I'd thought it a 'wet' poem: fairies and all that. Now I saw it differently. I saw a young knight, unhelmeted, with a white face like that of a poet with less than two years left to live.

'Don't just listen to the story,' said Mr Tosswill. 'Listen

to the *way* it's told. Why is it told that way, and not another way?'

We couldn't answer that. I doubt if he could answer it himself: if he had known *why*, surely he would have told us? But he had asked the question, the hardest question, the question few readers and teachers of poetry know – and dare – to ask. It would be years before I could answer it myself; before I understood that Keats's ballad stanza with the foreshortened fourth line was the perfect form for 'La Belle Dame', perfect because the dying fall of the foreshortened *line* – 'And no birds sing' – musically anticipates and confirms the story of a foreshortened *life*.

Tosswill (at last, I dare to drop the *Mr*) taught me many things: none more important, none for which I'm more grateful, than that the sound of a poem can be symbolic of the sense.

★

A year later – in the summer of 1950, when I was 15 – Tosswill stopped me as I was escaping from one of his classes and asked me a question: did I know Mr Geoffrey Keynes? I didn't.

'Well, he seems to know you, or at any rate he knows your father, and he's coming to give a talk on Rupert Brooke to the English Club next Friday. Would you like to come?' I said I would.

It seemed that the English Club (of which I'd never heard) met in his house after supper. I went along rather nervously, and my nervousness increased when I found that the members of the Club were all 'English specialists' of 17 or 18. I sat at the back and tried to look invisible.

Mr Tosswill introduced Mr Keynes as a Distinguished Old Rugbeian, friend of Rupert Brooke, Major in the First World War, Air Vice-Marshal in the Second, Consultant Surgeon at St Bartholomew's Hospital, Bibliographer of Jane Austen, William Blake, Sir Thomas Browne, John Donne, Thomas Fuller, Edward Gibbon, William Hazlitt, editor and author of many other books.

'This evening Mr Keynes has kindly agreed to speak to us about Rupert Brooke.' So saying, Mr Tosswill filled his pipe and withdrew into a cloud.

Mr Keynes, looking, I thought, more the Air Vice-Marshal (tall, lean, moustached) than the surgeon or the bibliographer (whatever that was), seemed embarrassed rather than flattered by his introduction. He spoke incisively but modestly: had been a very ordinary small boy, but lucky to have known Rupert Brooke. They were in the same house, School Field, and for years in the same form. Rupert would be at the top, Geoffrey at the bottom. When they'd a Greek or Latin translation for prep, Geoffrey would look up the words in Rupert's dictionary and the poet would weave them into elegant English. Deciding that his friend was a genius, Geoffrey soon began squirrelling away his manuscripts and Boswelling his conversation. But Rupert, he said, wasn't just clever and a poet. He played cricket and rugger for the school and, when he ran, his red-gold hair would flame out as if his head was on fire. He was also funny. People loved him because he made them laugh.

When they went to Cambridge – Geoffrey as an exhibitioner to Pembroke, Rupert as a scholar to King's – their friendship continued. Much of the Air Vice-Marshal's talk was an account of their meeting with Henry James, whom he and two friends invited to Cambridge for the weekend in the summer of 1909.

I'd never read a word of Henry James, but resolved to remedy that when I heard his letter of acceptance which Geoffrey Keynes read out:

My dear Triumvir,

  It's the most charming idea – that is, making my little visit June 11th is; & I beg you all (I like so that 'all' – such an affluence of flavour, yet without the taint of popularity!) to understand that I will gladly make it – your proposal – suit me. I have expected to be in town from May 1st to the end of the 1st week in June, & now I will stop over to the 11th for so beautiful a reason & come straight thence on that afternoon. So much for time. I only venture to make the most apologetic amendment as to place. Nothing could touch me more than your putting houses, in the Spanish manner, at my feet, but if I shan't seem too basely unappreciative it will suit me best that you kindly bespeak for me a good room &, if possible to be had, a sitting room at the ancient inn. It may be – that moment – for aught I know – your Commemorations week, or whatever name you give (pardon my indecent vagueness) the high festival – & rooms at inns much over-peopled. But by engaging it weeks ahead, the shelter I so invidiously invoke – may I not be able to count on it? This then is what I shall ask you very kindly to do. You see I am a more tattered and battered old person than you perhaps suppose & subject to interlunar swoons. But save during those discreet eclipses I shall be, my dear Triumvirate,

> Yours most truly,
> Henry James

Geoffrey and Rupert took James punting on the Cam, and when later someone told him that Rupert wrote poetry, which was no good, James is reported to have replied: 'Well, I must say I am *relieved*, for with *that* appearance if he had also talent it would be too unfair.' In due course, James discovered that Rupert *did* have talent and, in 1915, hearing of his death on the way to Gallipoli, he said 'Of course, of course,' and wept.

When Mr Keynes had finished and Mr Tosswill had emerged from his pestilential cloud to say that the speaker would take questions, I asked why Henry James had said 'Of course, of course'.

'The ancient Greeks had a saying,' Keynes replied, 'which Byron translated as "Whom the gods love die young."'

In bed that night it struck me: Keats had died at 25, Brooke at 28. Mightn't the gods love me? I began to feel doomed and important.

Next morning, I received a message: Mr Keynes wondered if I would have coffee with him after lunch. I, of course, said yes. He was staying in School Field and we took our coffee in the housemaster's chintzy sitting-room. The housemaster was also my form-master, and 'as a sheep before her shearers is dumb', I opened my mouth only to drink the coffee. Seeing my difficulty, Keynes suggested we take a turn round the Close and, as we walked under the elms, I think we were both on the lookout for a ghost with flaming hair.

Keynes said Tosswill had shown him the latest issue of *The New Rugbeian*, which contained three poems of mine, one of them called 'The Machine-Gun'. Why had I written that? I'd no idea. Had I ever seen a machine-gun? Yes, in the school cadet Corps. He told me of seeing machine-guns – and treating their victims – on the Western Front in the Great War. I began to feel uneasy about my poem and was glad when he changed the subject.

Would I like to come and see his Brooke – and other – books and manuscripts at Brinkley one weekend in the holidays? That was a question easily answered. He said he'd write and ask my parents if they could spare me. And he did.

*

In the old days, before Dr Beeching had filleted England of her railways, one could take a train from Liverpool Street that would pant to a halt at Six Mile Bottom, a dozen or so miles south-east of Cambridge. It and I arrived there late one afternoon in the summer of 1950, to be met by Geoffrey Keynes. He no longer had the air of an Air Vice-Marshal, but was wearing an open-necked shirt and was surprisingly unbuttoned, even boyish (though neither word would have occurred to me at the time), as he drove me back to Brinkley. Was I hungry? he asked. Jean had made a steak-and-kidney pie. Her steak-and-kidney pie was the best. Tomorrow he thought we might go round second-hand bookshops. Would I like that? Yes. Could I play croquet? No. He would teach me.

Geoffrey Keynes, I was to discover, had many gifts: not the least of them, a gift for friendship. An enthusiast himself, he was always on the lookout for enthusiasm in others and, to find this, would engage with them on their own terms. It was as natural for him to be boyish with a 15-year-old as to be gravely professional with grave professionals in any of his professions or avocations: surgery, bibliography, entomology, or mountaineering. He had an insatiable curiosity for the varieties of human experience and wanted to know how Jean made her steak-and-kidney pies or a 15-year-old his poems.

The address on the letter he'd sent my mother (handsomely printed in a sepia ink that matched his own) had been Lammas House, Brinkley, Newmarket, Suffolk, and turning into a broad backyard, he stopped the car some way short of the house.

'A blackbird's nesting in that pump under the kitchen window', he said, 'and we're trying not to disturb her.' Hospitality at Lammas House was absolute, as I began to understand at supper (it was, indeed, a supreme steak-and-kidney pie), forming a first impression of my hostess.

Margaret Keynes had been born Margaret Darwin, Charles Darwin's granddaughter, a member of the same intellectual galaxy as her husband's family with its interlinking constellations of Huxleys and Wedgwoods. No intellectual herself, she was earthy rather than galactic, green-fingered rather than blue-stockinged. In the Cambridge of the 1890s, Geoffrey Keynes had partnered Gwen Darwin (later, as Gwen Raverat, the author of *Period Piece*) at Miss Ratcliffe's Dancing Class, but he didn't partner the younger Miss Darwin until 1908. That summer, her father and her uncle together rented a crumbling Jacobean mansion, Vaynor Park in Montgomeryshire, for a family holiday, and Geoffrey was invited to join them. He was then a 21-year-old Cambridge undergraduate and Margaret an 18-year-old emerging from a schoolgirl's blue-serge chrysalis. They discovered a shared enthusiasm for the work of their local poet, and on long country walks would read to each other from Housman's *Shropshire Lad*:

Here of a Sunday morning
My love and I would lie,
And see the coloured counties,
And hear the larks so high
About us in the sky.

They met many times over the next six years, years in which Geoffrey fell in love with a young woman called Ka Cox, not knowing of her 'entanglement' (as he called it) with Rupert Brooke. He proposed, she refused him, and in August 1914 he was commissioned as a Lieutenant in the Royal Army Medical Corps. From Flanders, he wrote both to Ka and to Margaret and in due course sent each a handkerchief of Flanders lace. Ka's failed to change her mind, but Margaret's 'took' (Geoffrey's verb) – partly, I suspect, because she remembered that the warrior Othello's first gift to Desdemona had been such a handkerchief. Their courting was both complicated and spiced by the shortness of Geoffrey's leaves and the fact that Margaret had a secret job with Naval Intelligence.

Miss Ratcliffe's dancing class

Speaking of this after supper, in her Victorian sitting-room with the family silhouettes on the wall, her eyes sparkled – and Geoffrey's momentarily darkened at remembered indignity. One day after they'd lunched together, he insisted he was going to escort her back to her place of work, but Margaret had been sworn to secrecy. Pleading a natural necessity, she stopped at a hotel and, while he paced the foyer in mounting irritation and disbelief, she slipped out of the back door and scampered off to the Admiralty.

She was working as a junior cryptographer, decoding intercepted German messages, when one morning in June 1917 she was sent down to Room 40, the nerve-centre of Naval Intelligence, where they were in urgent need of extra help. The enemy had switched to a new and undeciphered code, and it was thought this might presage the emergence of their Fleet from the safety of Heligoland Bight, with potentially dangerous consequences for the Royal Navy.

Five or six young men in John Buchan tweeds, most of them Cambridge dons, were working at two tables. Several were smoking Meerschaum pipes, and their gloom was as palpable as the smoke surrounding them. Margaret's job was to copy out and tabulate their attempts at decipherment. These they categorized with the letters of the Greek alphabet, which she didn't know and spent her lunch-hours learning. They listened anxiously to every news bulletin, but there was no word of the German Fleet: only gains and losses on the Western Front and, one evening, a Zeppelin shot down on the Suffolk coast . . .

One of the young men called for a dispatch rider and gave him an order. He saluted, pulled down his goggles, and was gone. Next morning he returned and from his black satchel drew a charred piece of cardboard – a fragment of the Zeppelin's cipher-book – and that day the stubborn code was broken.

Geoffrey and Margaret were married in 1917. Thirty-three years and four sons later, they seemed to me masters of the art of living, and Lammas House their living masterpiece. If

Lammas House

'Margaret's room' was its heart, as she was the heart of the family, Geoffrey's study was its cerebellum. When guests were staying, coffee would be taken under the dark eyes of the Darwin silhouettes and then the men (and privileged boys) would withdraw to the study. Two walls of this carried glass-fronted bookcases containing the collector's treasure-hoard; a third held a fireplace and a constellation of paintings by William Blake; and the fourth opened into a bay window. There was a desk facing this and, in the middle of the room, a table at which Geoffrey usually worked. When entertaining a visitor, he would sit in a chair to the left of the fireplace, and the visitor in a chair to the right.

'What would you like to see?' he would say, in the voice of a genie prepared to produce rubies the size of cherries at the rub of a lamp, and was disappointed if you didn't reply: 'Keats's *Endymion*, 1818' or 'Sir Thomas Browne's *Hydriotaphia*, 1658'.

I'd never heard of most of his treasures and soon revealed I didn't even know that Blake was an artist as well as a poet, so my

Lammas education started there. Loose plates from *The Songs of Experience*, printed in blue or green by Blake himself, were put into my hand and, looking at these delicate miniatures, I recognized an old friend. But was this 'Tyger', pacing through the dim jungle, the same 'Tiger' I'd come to know caged in the white page of *The Dragon Book of Verse*? Yes and no. Certainly, meeting him in the different setting was a different experience. I began to be aware that the reading of a poem involves a simultaneous engagement of eye and ear: the eye attentive not only to the meaning of words, but to their grouping and spacing as lines on a page; the ear attuned to the grouping and spacing of sounds.

At the evening's end, I was allowed to take a facsimile of the *Songs* to study in bed, and Geoffrey, performing his day's last public ritual, took up a butler's tray of silver spoons to hide under his.

★

Lammas House, I learned, had many rituals. First, there was the tea-ceremony. Geoffrey would knock at one's door and enter wearing a dressing-gown with a tea tray in his hands. Resting this on the dressing-table, he would draw the curtains and tell you whether the mercury stem in his barometer had grown or shrunk in the night and what this meant the weather would do. Then, transferring his tray to the bed, he would pour the tea and unfold his plans for morning and afternoon.

Breakfast began with booksellers' catalogues. This ritual was seldom witnessed, because Geoffrey dressed and descended before Margaret and most guests. If one was down before nine, one found him abstracted, right hand twisting the gold ring on his left, or checking his watch until he could make the phone-calls that would bring down the 'bag' of the day.

There were outdoor as well as indoor rituals: for Margaret, the feeding of the hens; for Geoffrey, the visit to the Copse. This lay at the southern edge of their fifteen-acre property, and its trees

Geoffrey Keynes in his Copse

were his constant care – especially the *Metasequoia glyptostroboides* or Dawn Redwood, the 'fossil-tree' from Central China. He loved this as a father of a once-sickly child. It was a present from the Director of Kew Gardens and, soon after Geoffrey had planted it, a cow broke into the Copse and ate its leading stem. Fortunately, this was one branch of a **Y** and the skilled surgeon was able to splint and train the other branch to take over as leader. In 1950, when the *Metasequoia* and I were introduced, it was ramrod-straight and as tall as its master. Over the years of our friendship it grew another sixty feet.

There were always new trees to be planted in the Copse and always old trees to be pruned or felled. On my first visit, the trunk of a larch was waiting for the saw. Had I ever used a cross-cut? Geoffrey asked after breakfast. When I said yes, he looked doubtful, but a saw and an axe were collected from the work-shop and carried down to the Copse. I seemed to pass the first test satisfactorily; my father's training was commended; but when it was time for the axe, Geoffrey said that was Man's Work. Boys could build the bonfire. The branches were stacked before all the larch roundels had been split, and the tree-surgeon was clearly flagging.

'Couldn't I help? My father's taught me to use an axe, too.' Geoffrey again looked doubtful.

'You can try this easy one,' he said. It fell open as cleanly as a book.

'Not bad – for a poet,' he said. Taking turns with the axe, we finished splitting the logs and then lit – he lit – the bonfire.

'Boys these days can't light bonfires.' And when his one match had done its work: 'Would you know it was larch from the smell of the smoke?'

'No.'

'Different woods have different smells. Apple's the best. You must learn them.' I tried – during my forty-five years as under-woodsman at Lammas House – but wasn't an apt pupil. Thanks to Geoffrey, however, I did learn to taste the sweet smell of his balsam poplars every spring and the apple smoke of his fire every winter.

★

Jean was the jovial deity presiding over the Lammas kitchen. She gave us toad-in-the-hole and stewed plums for lunch: her toad-in-the-hole and his plums, Geoffrey said, were 'the best'; and I began to notice the regular recurrence of this superlative. Everything at Lammas, it seemed, was 'the best'. At first I was sceptical but, as the years passed without my meeting a more comfortable bed or better raspberries, I came to understand my host and hostess's infinite capacity for taking pains to secure the best for themselves and their friends. The best, I discovered, was by no means the same as the most expensive: on the contrary, they raised from seed plants that most people would buy in pots; and when Geoffrey wanted a soft-coloured wall to set off a peach tree, he bought a truck-load of ancient bricks from a collapsing country house and built it himself.

'I'm a craftsman,' he would say and the medial *s* made it the right word: the master-surgeon was a competent brick-layer, a good carpenter (responsible for much of the furniture in Lammas House and carved gate-posts in the garden), a distinguished editor, bibliographer, and book-collector. All these activities he saw as crafts, not to be confused with the higher and more visionary activity of the creative artist. He had his vanity – he knew he was a good craftsman (in some crafts 'the best') – but his formidable energies were directed by a deeper modesty in the service of other people: patients, friends, and artists.

He would say of his service to literature that it all began with Rupert Brooke, the first artist of his acquaintance; the first whose writings he collected; the first to tell him he should be reading John Donne (whose work, prior to Grierson's great edition of 1912, was known only to a few scholars). To read him, and then to bibliograph him, he had to buy his books. In the early days, these cost a few shillings; one of his two sixteenth-century manuscript collections of Donne's poems he bought from 'David's barrow' in Cambridge market for £5.

He built his library as he built his wall: book by book, brick by brick. In second-hand bookshop and sale-room, he became

the craftsman as hunter, and one of the pleasures of accompany-
ing him on such expeditions was hearing stories of the chase. My
favourite concerned *Mansfield Park*. In the course of compiling
the first edition of his bibliography of Jane Austen, Geoffrey had
seen in the world's great libraries copies of all her novels, except
Mansfield Park, 'in the original brown paper boards'. Had it been
published in that form? He could only speculate – until, one
sultry midsummer afternoon, he came upon a perfect copy 'in
the original brown paper boards' at the back of a country bookshop. It carried no price. The hunter made his plan. Muzzling
any sign of excitement, he continued his systematic beating of
the covers and then laid before the lady at the till a paperback
thriller, a contemporary novel (was it a Nevil Shute?), *Mansfield
Park*, and a gazetteer – stacked in that order.

She picked up the first, looked in the front, and wrote 6*d* on
her order-pad; picked up the second, looked in the front, and
wrote 2/–; picked up the third, looked in the front, looked in the
back, said 'Excuse me a moment', and left the room. He heard
her going upstairs. A bluebottle buzzed in the window. What
was to stop him leaving a £1 note on the counter and walking
out? He resisted the strong temptation.

She returned, wide-eyed, saying 'It's not known to Keynes!',
and wrote a large price (was it £50?) heavily on the fly-leaf. The
Unknown Bibliographer shuddered, dashed off a cheque, and
left before she could read his signature.

I think it was on my first outing as his gillie that he turned
from a bookshelf and said: 'Do you know the poems of John
Cornford?'

'No.'

'You should. I'll get you this. He was my godson.'

Driving home, he told me the story of Rupert John Cornford
– named after Rupert Brooke by Brooke's friends, Francis (the
philosopher) and Frances (the poet) Cornford – who had gone
to the Spanish Civil War carrying the revolver his father had
carried on the Western Front. Less fortunate than his father, he

was killed in the battle for Madrid either on his twenty-first birthday or the day after: someone else whom the gods had loved.

That night I took to bed the anthology, *Poems for Spain*, that Geoffrey had bought me – the first of many such educative presents – and reading John Cornford's dispatches from the Spanish Front, I was aware that others whom the gods loved were then on the march in Korea.

The last morning of my visit he showed me his collection of Brooke letters, manuscripts, and books. This included the corrected page proofs and two copies of *The Bastille*, Brooke's six-part poem that won the Rugby poetry prize in 1905.

'Does Rugby still have a poetry prize?' Geoffrey asked. I said I didn't know.

'Perhaps you should find out.'

★

While Geoffrey and I were in the study, Margaret would be outside. The garden was her daylight domain: its brilliant borders and 'tunnels of green gloom' complementing the scarlet and green morocco, the blue, brown, black, and gold of his shelves. It seemed to me inspired by Andrew Marvell's poem 'The Garden' (to which I had been admitted in Geoffrey's large folio first edition):

> What wondrous life is this I lead!
> Ripe apples drop about my head;
> The luscious clusters of the vine
> Upon my mouth do crush their wine;
> The nectarine and curious peach
> Into my hands themselves do reach;
> Stumbling on melons, as I pass,
> Ensnared with flowers, I fall on grass.
>
> Meanwhile the mind, from pleasure less
> Withdraws into its happiness;
> The mind, that Ocean where each kind

Does straight its own resemblance find;
Yet it creates, transcending these,
Far other worlds and other seas
Annihilating all that's made
To a green thought in a green shade.

In all such gardens one expects a serpent, and in the Keynes's it was the Spirit of Croquet. I was as innocent as Adam, and my Fall from Innocence into Experience was painful. While the hateful hoops seemed to have a magnetic attraction for my host's ball, mine they repelled, though not as far or as fast as Geoffrey propelled it whenever we coincided.

Only in the train home did it strike me that one of the reasons for the Keynes's harmonious marriage was the fact that Margaret neither collected books nor played croquet.

★

Returning in September to Rugby and the lesser ferocity of the rugger field, I was soon on the wrong side of the sidelines again, but was brought back into play by a master who converted a slow wing-three-quarter into a fast wing-forward, a marauder of the middle air between the higher realm of the winged heels and the infernal regions of the scrum. In that role I played for the school's Young Guard under-16, but my lack of weight again began to tell and I descended to the nether regions, taking my place in the front row of the scrum. I became a hooker, the player whose foot strikes at the ball as it enters the tunnel between the two packs of forwards, once the opposing front rows have locked heads as fighting bulls lock horns. His principal job is to 'hook' it into the back of the scrum, where it can be deployed in an attacking manoeuvre. With practice, I developed some skill at this, and for eight autumns enjoyed the fellowship of the scrum.

In those years – perhaps because I was fit and buoyant – autumn was also the season when I harvested poems. Acting on Geoffrey Keynes's hint, I asked about the school poetry prize and found that entries of not less than 200 lines were solicited on the subject of 'The Golden Years'. The only years of which I knew anything being my own, I planned a poem that would trace the only golden thread I could think of through those years. A 'dream vision' (owing something to Langland's *Piers Plowman*) of encounters with characters from my favourite books began to take shape. Following a river from its source – recognizably a spring on Shotover – my speaker found, first, a skiff carrying a toad and a water-rat; then, a trussed-up Gulliver, a Pied Piper turning a tide of rats, Don Quixote assaulting a windmill, Sir Galahad felling a Red Knight, Captain Silver and Blind Pew, Christian climbing to a golden city, and finally, on the summit of another hill, another swordsman.

> His eyes were shielded with a weathered hand,
> And when at length I gained the rocky ledge
> I saw, below, a white-lipped fringe of sand –
> Beyond, the sea.

'I' asked his name. He said 'Men call me Cortez.' (I didn't know that Keats's sonnet 'On First Looking into Chapman's Homer' credited the wrong conquistador.)

At his side, my Golden Yearling ended on what he meant to be a high note:

> I looked across the plains of fantasy,
> Back to the blue hills of the rising sun,
> Where Youth's small spring of cloudless ecstasy
> Breaks from the cool sands of oblivion.
> But greater waters now are calling me
> To tranquil deeps and whirlpools of despond;
> And I must set my tiller to the sea
> To seek the sunset and the lands beyond.

My mother strenuously objected to the whirlpools of despond, on the grounds that despond was a state of mind into which

no good Christian could fall. After one of our rare arguments,
I rubbed out the offending phrase, but restored it some days later
(whether from an overdue assertion of independence, or an
inability to find another rhyme, I can't tell). I cannot see into the
mind of that 15-year-old, but can follow the one-finger typing
of a fair copy on his father's Imperial, its binding in a brown paper
cover, and hopeful posting. It won the prize – causing some
merriment because the Head of the School was runner-up – and
was returned with pencilled marginalia in a recognizable hand.
Arthur fforde had again marked some patterns of assonance, and
opposite the closing lines had written two and a half stanzas of
an Italian poem, underlining the words '*Voi altri pochi*' and adding
'See *Paradiso*, Canto II'. When I did so, I found them translated:
'*Ye other few* . . . ye may indeed commit your vessel to the deep'.

That authorization played no part in my parents' decision to
cross the Channel that summer and rent a house in the Breton
fishing port of Camaret. My sisters and I swam and explored the
cliffs with Jacqueline, a beautiful French girl, who was living
nearby. Her brown ankles danced into a poem that tried to do
justice to their rhythms – and the metrics of a night in which
pedestrian iambic pentameters had no place:

CAMARET EN FÊTE (AUGUST, 1951)

There was dancing by night and singing by day
Down in the streets of Camaret;
And the fishing-boats along the quay
Rode at their anchors silently,
While the hammers were still in the building yard
And the nets lay idle on the hard.
But up in the town there was eating and drinking
With rattle of knives and glasses clinking.
The tavern doors were opened wide
And laughter and shouting raged inside
As the landlord hastened to and fro
With bottles of cider and red Bordeaux:

And the children came out when the sun went down
To light the lanterns round the town.

Then a fiddle struck up in the market square
And the Breton girls with flowers in their hair
Came dancing down between high grey walls
In their coloured scarves and tasselled shawls,
With full skirts whirling, on the night wind blown
And the frill of a petticoat sometime shown
As bare brown ankles rising, falling,
Awoke the echoes and set them calling
With rattle of clogs on the cobbles beating;
As wheeling, checking, advancing, retreating,
In a torrent of greens and blues and reds
With swaying hips and nodding heads
They swept through the streets of Camaret,
Down past the church and along the bay,
Where caught in a mesh of dark tackle and spars
Hung a floundering moon and captive stars.

The old folk sat in the lanterns' glow,
Recalling days when long ago
They too had danced the night away
Here in the streets of Camaret;
But now in their berets and tall lace caps
With their children's children in their laps
They spoke of days in a thoughtful vein,
Whose like would never be seen again.
The curé was there in his shovel hat
(That he evermore left where he last had sat)
And he picked up his skirts and joined the throng,
Singing with his flock as they moved along.
So they danced round the harbour and they danced up the hill –
When the clock struck three they were dancing still,
And at length when their feet could scarcely stand,
Went dancing homeward, hand in hand.

So the east grew warm with returning day
And a spinney of masts rose out of the bay

As the sun appeared from a couch of clouds,
And climbing aloft by the mizzen shrouds
It looked disconsolately down
On the smokeless roofs of the sleeping town.
Not a shutter was open, but in the square
While the wind's light fingers teased his hair,
The fiddler slept on a bench in the middle,
His white head pillowed upon his fiddle,
Dreaming he played at the courts of heaven . . .
The cocks were crowing (for 'twas well past seven)
When the old man rose, and brushing the dew
From his broad black hat turned homeward too.

As he climbed the hill beneath him lay
The sunlit port of Camaret;
But the quay was clear where the nets had dried
For the fishing-fleet sailed on the five o'clock tide.

The best that can be said for this is that it owes more to Life
than Literature (unlike 'The Golden Years'); although, ironically,
I was persuaded by Mr Tosswill – who proclaimed the former
more important than the latter – to introduce the inert literary
word 'evermore' in place of my own 'always'.

*

We returned to England to find that 'greater waters' were calling
us all. My father was offered a Visiting Professorship for some
months the following year at the Royal Prince Alfred Hospital
in Sydney. His decision – reached rapidly, like all his decisions –
revealed his priorities: he would go if his family could go with
him. But how would his children's schools react to the suggestion that they should miss a term? With horror: 'loss of
concentration . . . stability . . . chance of scholarships . . . relationship with staff and contemporaries'.

'Nonsense,' said my father (to all those propositions); then
cabled his acceptance of the Professorship, and booked three
cabins on the RMS *Orion*.

One loss did concern me: that of a rugger term, but there would be other rugger terms and there might never be another chance to see 'the round earth's imagined corners' – particularly its Australasian corners – or, to reverse John Donne's metaphor, to see the flat map fleshed out with its mountains and forests, rivers and seas. My sisters thought that any scheme involving a term's absence from school must be a good scheme. My mother, whose memories of rounding the Horn in mid-winter were still painfully clear, didn't relish the prospect of a sea voyage without the support of my father, who was to fly out later, but had the consolation that her brother, Ruskin, would also be on the *Orion*, returning from a holiday in Europe with his wife and son.

·

5

Dinnschenchas

[Placename-lore]

ON 18 AUGUST 1952, we struggled up the gang-plank of the great white liner with our suitcases and were soon entering the Channel with a movement very different from that of John Masefield's 'Dirty British coaster . . . Butting through the Channel in the mad March days' or, to my mother's relief, the old *Port Sydney* limping towards London.

Last thing at night in my narrow bunk, I wrote up my 'log' of the day's events. Reading this almost fifty years later, I'm struck by its tedious accumulation of trivial detail and, more surprisingly, by its failure – at what seem now significant moments – to give an account of the origin of what have since become crucial memories. This raises the question of whether they are true memories or false, and though I cannot prove them true in point of detail, I cannot believe them false, given their relation to what one might call the 'imaginative truth' of their context.

After two and a half days at sea, I was on deck, watching for a particular sea-mark:

Nobly, nobly, Cape Saint Vincent to the North-west died away;
Sunset ran, one glorious blood-red, reeking into Cádiz Bay;
Bluish 'mid the burning water, full in face Trafalgar lay . . .

Browning saw it on a better day.

As morning drew into afternoon, dark rocks crowded in on us and the channel narrowed; but, with the first winds of evening, Spain and Africa fell away and we passed from one world into another. All that had gone before – the rain-swept wharves of Tilbury, the blurred faces and fluttering handkerchiefs, the mirrored lights of the great harbour, the arc-lamps guiding us through the lock and out to sea, the Bay of Biscay and the ragged coast of Portugal – all were forgotten, so impressive was the sight ahead. The Rock of Gibraltar rose from a sea as tranquil and unruffled as the sky above it, and in its shadow we dropped anchor for the first time.

To everyone's disappointment, only disembarking passengers were allowed ashore. After supper, I went on deck to hear the Rock, like a crouching lion, roar its defiance towards Spain; gun-batteries sending salvo after salvo of scarlet 'star-shells' chasing each other down a lighthouse beam. They bounced off the water, skimming, bouncing and skimming, bouncing and skimming into the darkness. After this imperial fireworks display, I was taking a tour round the deck when I recognized two dark figures, arm in arm at the rail, gazing towards Gibraltar: my mother and my uncle. I was about to speak to them when I realized they needed to be alone with their memories of their brother Bill, buried in a grave they had never seen and could not see, perhaps only a few hundred yards away.

I follow the flight of the star-shells in my log, but make no mention of the victim of such shelling on beaches to the east. Was I then unaware of his proximity? Have I invented his brother and sister's dark vigil (memory, I know, has its creative faculty)? Perhaps I omitted them out of respect for the privacy of grief and for fear of distressing my mother should she read my log. I cannot believe that she and Ruskin weren't thinking of their older – and at the same time younger – brother, as the gun-batteries thundered above his grave.

Two days' sailing through a gale brought us to the Bay of Naples and its seething city, brilliant with flowering oleanders and advertisements. We sampled the hectic life of its streets and squares, and took a bus out to the very different streets and squares of Pompeii. I had read Pliny's account of the eruption of Vesuvius in AD 79, and would take back indelible images of a dog in its death agony, a seated man covering his eyes, 'cast' by archaeologists in plaster of Paris pumped into cavities left by decomposed bodies in the volcanic ash that buried them.

My experience of Gibraltar and those Pompeian casts made me more responsive to the memorial to the New Zealand and Australian Royal Mounted Rifles at Port Said than to the immense stone statue of De Lesseps, architect of the Suez Canal into which we steamed on 27 August. If the voyage had set me thinking seriously about death for the first time, it was also teaching me more about varieties of life than I had learnt in several years at school.

A high proportion of our fellow passengers on the *Orion* were recently retired Australians, returning from holidays in England with new dentures, hearing-aids, and spectacles (provided free by the National Health Service), but there were also some younger ones with whom we played deck tennis and swam in the ship's pool by day and danced away the tropical nights. There was Ann, who brought me to my senses on a tilting dance-floor, and Murray, who swam like an otter and would win four gold medals in the 1956 Olympics. There were also the nameless ones with dark faces and bright clothes at every port we came to – Aden, Colombo, the Cocos Islands. What did they make of the nameless paler faces descending the gang-plank from the floating hotel? Not until later did the question occur to me.

My father was on the Sydney quay to meet us in the third week of September, and some days later was waving to us again as the SS *Manowai* cast off her moorings and headed for New Zealand.

Arriving in Wellington, we were folded to the hospitable bosom of my mother's family. Over the coming weeks, I would shake the hands of (among others) fifty-two cousins, mostly identified in my log, but here again log and memory part company. Merlyn was the cousin I remember best – for three reasons: she was very attractive, both beautiful and vivacious; she was passionate about poetry and, indeed, engaged to a poet; and she was dying of consumption. I can remember my father telling me this and replying to my protest – 'But she has such a beautiful complexion!' – that this was a poignant characteristic of those in her condition. My log, however, makes no mention of her illness. Why? Once again, perhaps, I was worried that my notebook might fall into other hands.

What it does record are our conversations about poetry. Merlyn and her fiancé, Mike Doyle, introduced me to a body of work that I (in my insular ignorance) had not known existed: New Zealand poetry. This, they showed me, had three distinct strata: first, the poetry of Englishmen written in New Zealand; second, the poetry about New Zealand by people (mainly men) torn between an old tradition and a new one 'struggling to be born'; and third, the new voice of a new country.

Merlyn was enthusiastic about the first poet to speak with that new voice, Ursula Bethell (1874–1945), and showed me her poem, 'Detail':

> My garage is a structure of excessive plainness,
> It springs from a dry bank in the back garden,
> It is made of corrugated iron,
> And painted all over with brick-red.
>
> But beside it I have planted a green Bay-tree,
> – A sweet Bay, an Olive, and a Turkey Fig,
> – A Fig, an Olive, and a Bay.

My aunts and uncles spoke of England as 'Home' – even if they had never been there – but Bethell's 'Detail' spoke of another and more genuine home (with a lower-case h) as distinctly as Betjeman's poems spoke of North Oxford. The celebration both of her structure's 'excessive plainness' and her far-from-plain planting beside it – realism balanced by Romance (lower-case garage, upper-case Fig, Olive, and Bay) – captured perfectly the relationship between New Zealand's urban and natural land-scape. Bethell's was a 'poetry of place', but there were figures in her landscape and she spoke of both in a voice confident, lyrical, and humane:

> It would not be a hard thing to wake up one morning
> to sound of bird-song in scarce-stirring willow-trees,
> waves lapping, oars splashing, chains running slowly,
> and faint voices called across the harbour;
> to embark at dawn, following the old forefathers,
> to put forth at daybreak for some lovelier,
> still undiscovered shore.

I found the same blend of realism and Romance, confident relaxation and control, in the work of the best of Bethell's suc-cessors, as, for example, in James K. Baxter's 'Wild Bees':

> Often in summer on a tarred bridge plank standing
> Or downstream between willows, a safe Ophelia drifting
> In a rented boat – I had seen them come and go,
> Those wild bees swift as tigers, their gauze wings a-glitter
> In passionless industry, clustering black at the crevice
> Of a rotten cabbage tree, where their hive was hidden low.
>
> But never strolled too near. Till one half-cloudy evening
> Of ripe January, my friends and I
> Came, gloved and masked to the eyes like plundering
>   desperadoes
> To smoke them out. Quiet beside the stagnant river
> We trod wet grasses down, hearing the crickets chitter
> And waiting for light to drain from the wounded sky.
>
> Before we reached the hive their sentries saw us
> And sprang invisible through the darkening air;
> Stabbed, and died in stinging. The hive woke. Poisonous
>   fuming

Of sulphur filled the hollow trunk, and crawling
Blue flame sputtered: yet still their suicidal
Live raiders dived and clung to our hands and hair.

O it was Carthage under the Roman torches
Or loud with flames and falling timber, Troy.
A job well botched: half of the honey melted
And half the rest young grubs. Through earth-black
    smouldering ashes
And maimed bees groaning, we drew out our plunder –

Little enough their gold, and slight our joy.
Fallen then the city of instinctive wisdom.
Tragedy is written distinct and small:
A hive burned on a cool night in summer.
But loss is a precious stone to me, a nectar
Distilled in time, preaching the truth of winter
To the fallen heart that does not cease to fall.

I envied these poets the new world, new places, proclaimed
in their titles – 'Waitaki Dam', 'A View of Rangitoto' – and the
new words for the flora and fauna flourishing beside their
garages: cabbage tree and mānuka, bell-bird and tui. This was
their home, but I had to accept it wasn't mine. Riding the
boundary fences of an uncle's sheep-station, reeling in the
salmon-trout from Lake Taupo, I was a privileged visitor. At
Rotorua, among geysers and farting mud-pools, or in the
Waitomo caves lit by a million glow-worms, I was a tourist.
Admiring Maori war-canoes, clubs, spears, and tikis in the
Wellington museum, I came to the sorrowful realization that a
history I had claimed at the Dragon could never be mine.

I did feel a faint charge of ancestral electricity in the
Wellington Parliament buildings, where a grandfather and great-
grandfather had strutted and fretted their hour upon the stage,
and walking with my mother through the dark rooms of
'Glenorchy'. Her father's big chair was still in its rightful place,
but it was empty and I began to sense that, important as place

would be to me and to my poems, people would be more important. My other grandfather came with us – on the ferry and over
the hills – to Dargaville. We visited the kauri forest, in whose
ceremonial hand-over to the nation the old man and his Boy
Scout son had taken part; the jetty from which that boy had
fished in the broad brown river; and further north, the seventy-
mile beach where they had swum and dug for toaroa shellfish.
Again I felt a charge of ancestral electricity, but again the lighthouse of imagination remained unlit.

On 29 November, we boarded the SS *Rangitoto*, named after
the mountain that shrank into our wake as we sailed out of
Auckland Harbour into a heavy sea. For me, the horizon was
clouded by the news in a letter from my Rugby house-tutor
that, if I was to sit for a Magdalen scholarship, it would have to
be in English *and French*, and that I therefore had three months
in which to acquire 'a comprehensive knowledge of French literature'. Despite ten years of expensive schooling and several
holidays in France, my grasp of French – both written and
spoken – was tenuous. I knew I had no chance of a scholarship,
but hoped for a 'commoner's' place on the (relative) strength of
my scholarship papers, and to that end had combed the
Auckland bookshops for an *Oxford Book of French Verse*, the plays
of Molière, Rousseau's *Confessions*, and Voltaire's *Candide*. I
tried to give my mind – I couldn't give my heart – to these and
other masterpieces as the *Rangitoto* ploughed her lonely furrow
across the Pacific, but there were too many distractions: swimming races in the ship's pool and games of deck-quoits with my
father, the sighting of a water-spout or flying fish, and then the
lifting and lowering of the ship in the locks of the Panama
Canal. Christmas Day found us in the South Atlantic out of
which, four days later, rose the lights of Southampton and we
were home – or, as my aunts and uncles would have put it –
Home.

★

On 18 January, my eighteenth birthday, I returned to Rugby with less than a month in which to perfect my comprehensive knowledge of English and French literature. During those weeks, I communed with almost no one apart from a faithful fag, who kept me supplied with tea and toast, and the Great Dead. The papers I then wrote gained me a place (no doubt by a narrow margin) at Magdalen College, Oxford.

More educative than my weeks of cramming were those the school authorities organized as a course in civics for 'Leavers' who had finished their exams. We helped a local farmer bring in his winter potatoes, tugging them out of the frozen ground until our fingers bled and our backs ached. We hurtled down the shaft of a coal-mine and swung shovels in hot galleries where again our fingers bled and our backs ached. Having learnt a salutary lesson about how some other people lived and earned a livelihood, we were taken to a magistrates' court and sat in a more comfortable gallery to hear witnesses give widely divergent accounts of the same traffic accidents. 'What is truth? said jesting Pilate; and would not stay for an answer.' I began to see why.

★

Awaiting my return to Shotover for the Easter holidays was a now-routine letter from Bruno, editor of *The Draconian*, asking for Rugby news. Over the past two years I'd sent him dispatches in the couplet codes of Chaucer, Pope, and Walter Scott, and responded to this latest request with an updated version of Dryden's 'Absalom and Achitophel':

> In peaceful times ere Reuter did begin,
> Before invention was accounted sin,
> When Bruno prompted and no law attacked
> Promiscuous use of fantasy and fact,
> There dwelt in Rugby's many-factioned throng

A band yet noble though in size less strong
Than in the high days it had known before.
Where had been thirty now remained a score
Of which their correspondent stood the first –
A name to every news-concealer curst
For crooked wiles and nagging without pause –
Who on his wailed return from southern shores
Performed in first fifteen and running eight
And passed to Oxford. His unbridled hate,
When moved to speech, he curbs by slow degrees
And sheds his venom in such words as these.

'Titles and names 'tis tedious to rehearse
Of those beneath the dignity of verse,
Yet honour burgeons in the Dragon band,
In the first rank of which does Raisman stand,
Who in the course of one revolving moon
Played hockey, golf, and led his house platoon;
Then acted as Tartuffe and waxing grim
Beat Guinness, thinking 'it was good for him'.
This last, undaunted, yet achieved success
In classics and the under-sixteen chess.'

And so on, for another fifty lines. This exercise warmed me up
for something more ambitious, a variation on another Old
Masterpiece, prompted by evensong in the chapel of King's
College, Auckland. I was still at the age and stage when art students draw from casts and copy Leonardos; a necessary and
healthy stage, not always seen as such by reviewers who criticize
young authors for revealing influences, forgetting the traces of
Blake in early Yeats, traces of Yeats in early Larkin, traces of
Larkin in the early work of many poets since.

I doubt if I remembered reading Arnold's 'Rugby Chapel'
shortly before going to Rugby or saw any symmetry in adopting his title for a poem written shortly before leaving. Where
Arnold's was an elegiac tribute to 'the Doctor', his father, mine
was a tribute to him and another poet whose plaque I had first

seen with the doctor, *my* father. Dr Arnold had owned land —
and seen one of his sons settle — in New Zealand, and at the start
of my poem I tried to unite my own experience of the two
countries I had thought of as mine:

I

Now at the tide's turn in unnumbered bays
   The long wave's wash steals back across the sand,
And breakers dwindle into foam. The day's
   Blue depths, illumined where shaft-sunbeams stand,
Ebb between stars down roadsteads of the sky . . .
   Deep grasses whiten as a wind dips by;
While seemingly uplifted from the land
   The whale's back of King's chapel curves, to lie
Athwart a cloud-reef of pink coral, stranded high.

II

The darkness settles round me, and once more
   A wind made sweet with mānuka descends
From Rangitoto the great mountain's shore;
   And low above the dim field's quiet ends
Leaps up the moon, whose tinsel touch extends
   To every leaf upon the rimu tree,
And to the windows of the chapel lends
   A mist of mellow gold. Then strong and free
Break out the bells for evensong and summon me.

III

So at the bat's hour from a windy Close
   The bell-surge bids another school arise,
And leads them where the great East window glows
   And Rugby Chapel, all-perceiving, lies,
Its blunt tower brooding on tumultuous skies.
   So comes the old world sudden to the new
And things remembered, till the vision dies,
   Stand closer than those present and more true.
King's chapel doors lay open and I wandered through.

My mistake was to put New Zealand wine into an old bottle, choosing – probably for no better reason than that I hadn't used it before – the nine-line stanza Spenser devised for *The Faerie Queene*. I had yet to learn that a good marriage of form to content is an essential element in any successful poem, and a *bad* marriage (as here) is a reason for the failure of countless unsuccessful poems. My use of Spenser's deliberately archaic model led me to overlook the archaism of 'Athwart a cloud-reef of pink coral, stranded high'.

Why didn't I use the unrhymed and more 'open form' of Arnold's poem? I had tried writing free verse at Rugby and didn't like the result: something else I had still to learn was that, with rare exceptions, the poets who write successfully in open forms – Pound, Eliot, Lawrence, Auden, Plath – have first written successfully in closed forms.

Entering King's chapel doors, my imagination returned to Rugby chapel, hymn-books and psalters laid out along the ledges of the pews – 'On each alternate title-page a new name signed':

XXX

> This, some will leave with others that have gone
>   Arrayed in honour to the far unknown;
> As he whose ageless features yet live on,
>   Their light imparted to enduring stone:
> And though at last all here be overthrown,
>   Time shall not conquer nor the years subdue
> His gifted utterance, who sleeps alone
>   Where Skyros olives murmur the night through
> And clouds blow high in heavens of Ægean blue.

For better or (many will think) for worse, Rupert Brooke had a high place in my schoolboy pantheon.

★

Like every other boy who was to leave school that summer, I was thinking how best to spend the mandatory two-year National Service. Richard Sorabji and other of my academically more able contemporaries were signing up for the Russian courses offered by the Army and Navy, but that option didn't appeal to me. After more than a decade of classrooms, I wanted a change. Remembering Dr Johnson's dictum that 'Every man thinks meanly of himself for not having been a soldier', I inquired about the possibility of a commission in the Oxfordshire and Buckinghamshire Light Infantry and was provisionally accepted as a Second Lieutenant, subject to satisfactory performance at Officers' Training School. Shortly afterwards, however, two friends of mine destined for the same regiment heard depressing accounts of the rigours of a subaltern's life in the British Army of the Rhine, with which the Ox. and Bucks. was then serving. We asked to be seconded to a battalion of the King's African Rifles about to be trained in Tanganyika, prior to active service in Malaya. Had we asked to be seconded to West Africa, no doubt we would have been sent to East. As it was, we were told that, if all went well, we would be seconded to the Royal West African Frontier Force. I thought this had a gratifyingly Kiplingesque ring to it but, with the imminent approach of my last summer term, didn't have time to open an atlas and find what frontiers there were to enforce.

The only books I opened that term were books of poetry and novels. Since I usually opened them beside the swimming pool or at the edge of a cricket field (we were Cock-House at cricket that summer), little of their contents was digested. My only task was – with a friend and fellow 'English specialist', David Cocks – to edit *The New Rugbeian*. The fact that it was the Coronation Number solved the problem of the editorial and made it easier to coax advertising revenue out of loyal hosiers and hoteliers. All that remained was to coax copy out of our friends and neighbours and, when that was inadequate, to fill the gaps ourselves – David, with a good story, his co-editor with a poem called (God knows why) 'Perpetua':

They have laid my love between four wax candles
   In a coffin of cedar wood with lilies in her hair;
And the four flames burn in the bier's bright handles,
   Each like a cherub's hands arched in prayer.

★ ★ ★

At dusk they found her, like a wild swan sleeping,
   Amid the scattered poppies she had gathered from the wheat,
Dreaming of dawns beyond the long days reaping
   With flame-winged petals upon her feet.

In white they veiled her as bride for her wedding
   And bore her to the chapel in a dew-embroidered dress,
With the quiet trees of the green ride shedding
   A random leaf at her loveliness.

★ ★ ★

A tall flame dies and its fellow lights falter
   As winds about her jostle with the shadows on the stone,
But nothing hereafter the calm can alter
   Of these folded hands we thought our own.

'I pray you lift the linen that hides her face –
   Most strange it is that she, who seems so little when confined,
She that of her stature filled so small a space,
   Should leave, in passing, such void behind.'

'No, kiss her not again now lest she waken,
   But lay the cloths upon her face, and softly let us go.
Death must love this bride that he has taken –
   Let her sleep on: she is happier so.'

This suggests that the books over which I had dozed beside pool and cricket pitch included those of the Rossettis and Swinburne. More interestingly, however, I can see now something I couldn't see then. My Pre-Raphaelite fantasy of Love and Death is a subconscious response to the marriage – shortly after we left New Zealand – and imagined death of my cousin Merlyn.

The New Rugbeian was published in June, on the weekend of
the School Dance, a principal topic of conversation for weeks
before and weeks after: whom to ask as one's partner; where she
would stay; if with one's housemaster, whether he and his wife
were heavy sleepers. Only the last of these questions concerned
me. I had long ago invited Angela (appropriately named, since
she had the face and figure of a Pre-Raphaelite angel), whom I
had met at a dance in Oxford. She had accepted and it was agreed
that she would share my housemaster's guest room with some
other imported beauties.

Of the dance itself I remember only a general sense of exhilar-
ated exaltation – owing more to her company than the 'cider
cup' – and some surprise at not being disappointed by our deco-
rous behaviour. We had 'world enough and time' for . . . what?
I doubt if either of us could have given much of an answer
to that question. The following day, in Angela's fragrant wake,
I began the last poem I would write at Rugby:

School Dance

Laughing into the night they come,
    Their hands a knot this dark shall not undo;
Some that shall see their battles out, and some
    As certain that shall not come through.

We from the darkness watch them pass
    Hearing their blown talk, and above the band
The sighing of girls' dresses on the grass,
    And the wind over the long land.

So, laughing, shall the couples come
    Flushed from their dancing when our feet are gone:
While diamond-eyed, but in their mercy dumb,
    Still the omniscient stars burn on.

The years hold forth no hope for these –
    Regret nor joy can lie within their range,
Who gleam as fretted coral from dim seas,
    Passive beyond the chance of change.

Look not to them, though they be wise,
  But live the moment to its natural end,
And in the transient glory of girls' eyes
  Forget what soon the stars may send.

I doubt if I sent this to Angela.

Then the last packing and unpacking of the school trunk; a last report for Bruno ('The text of "Kubla Khan" as recently emended and revised at Rugby'); and time to search the Shotover atlas for the frontiers of the pink pieces of the West African jigsaw.

★

On 1 October 1953, my mother drove me to the gates of Cowley Barracks, the Oxfordshire and Buckinghamshire Light Infantry depot, less than a mile from the foot of Shotover Hill. Passing through the gates, I joined a queue of other nervous 18-year-olds and was given a number, a 'bed space' in a barrack-room, 'eating irons' (knife, fork, spoon, mug, plate), a full set of 'webbing' (belt, ammunition pouches, haversack, gaiters), and a uniform (beret to boots). After supper, an awesome personage in a dark green uniform with a scarlet sash appeared in our barrack-room. Like a priest about to serve mass, he lit a candle on the table and laid out his sacraments or instruments under a yellow cloth. Turning then to face his huddled congregation, he introduced himself as Colour-Sergeant Oxborough, come to introduce us to an infantryman's best friends – his boots. He introduced us to his own. They were objects of great beauty, their toe-caps reflecting the shifting candle-light but, he told us, once they'd been as dull and dimpled as those with which we'd just been issued. What had transformed them? He would show us, but for this would need a volunteer. Who would entrust him with one of his best friends?

I already had a friend in the barrack-room, called Julian. Assessing the situation more rapidly than the rest of us, he offered up one of his lustreless twins. The colour-sergeant inserted his left hand into it and, with his right, produced a spoon from under the yellow cloth. This he held in the candle-flame for a minute or two; then, raising it towards his mouth, spat on it. The spoon spat back, and very gently he began to rub its curved back round and round over the boot's dull and dimpled toe-cap. Coming closer, we watched the miracle: like warts under the hand of a faith-healer, the dimples disappeared. When the toe-cap was scoured smooth, the colour-sergeant exchanged his spoon for a bone toothbrush and, holding this the wrong way round, with the rounded tip of the handle began rubbing spittle and Kiwi boot-polish into the now corpse-grey leather. 'It has to be a *bone* toothbrush,' he said, 'and it has to be *Kiwi* boot-polish' (the New Zealander in me was obscurely gratified by this). After an hour or so, he gave Julian back a boot with the beginnings of a shine on its toe-cap, saying 'That'll do for tonight. I'll finish it tomorrow.'

The following evening he returned – to a congregation with uniformly cropped heads and sore right arms (from a cocktail of injections) – and the baptism of the boot resumed. Another hour of spit and polish concluded with the caress of the yellow duster and the presentation of an object of great beauty to its proud owner.

For many evenings after, we lit our candles and administered the sacraments to our best friends, but they didn't respond as Julian's had to the hands of the High-Priest. This was a source of sorrow to us all and to no one more than Julian, who on every parade would be harshly interrogated about his ''orrible left boot'. This was no more 'orrible than others in the squad, but beside its brilliant twin it looked blind. A boot that had been the envy of us all became a torment to poor Julian.

The danger of volunteering in the Army was the first of many lessons learnt in that barrack-room. For me, they continued the schooling of Naples and Colombo, the potato-field and the mine. My immediate neighbour, Richard, was a strange boy, whose behaviour became stranger as the days passed. He was the 'awkward one' in any squad, turning left when others turned right, seemingly unable to understand the simple mechanism of the rifle. Rejecting all conversational overtures, he would answer direct questions with a monosyllable, but otherwise was totally silent. Every day, he got up to shave at three in the morning and, whenever we were not on parade, would sit cross-legged on his bed reading the same small book. He wouldn't tell us what it was. The baptism of the boot appeared beyond his powers, but he was rescued by Tom – a hard case with a prison record – who for two days put in as much work on Richard's best friends as on his own. Julian and I and another public-schoolboy in the room were content to play Levite to Tom's Good Samaritan.

Tom withdrew his help, however, when it became clear that Richard was refusing to help himself, and the question was no longer whether – but when – the sword of Damocles would fall. We didn't have long to wait for an answer. In the hours before our first kit inspection, the barrack-room was seething with activity – except in one corner. While the rest of us were polishing boots and brass buckles, or arranging haversacks and ammunition pouches in their prescribed tiers, at the foot of each bed, Richard was still sitting cross-legged on his unmade bed, reading his little book. At the dreaded command 'Stand by your beds', we leaped to attention – all except Richard, who simply put his book under his pillow and stood up. The inspecting officer entered the room preceded by a colour-sergeant, who moved ahead of him, running a laser eye up and down each recruit and his bed-space, straightening a crooked cap-badge, brushing a flake of dandruff off a trembling shoulder. Reaching Richard, he said in a low gritty voice, like that of a diamond cutting glass: 'What's wrong with your bed?'

'You can see, can't you?' said Richard. 'It's not made.'

'Then you'd better make it.'

'Make it yourself!' Richard replied.

The pane of glass snapped and the little mutineer was marched

out to the guardroom so fast his feet seemed not to touch the
floor.

We learned later he was a pacifist Elim Pentecostal. As soon
as this was established, he was discharged, leaving me to reflect
on the greatest act of courage I would witness during my two
years in the Army.

After a month's 'basic training', we were allowed out of barracks, for the first time (apart from a supervised afternoon on a
rifle-range), on a cross-country run. Since it was 'my' country
we would be crossing, and much drilling and tumbling over
assault-courses had made me very fit, I looked forward to this as
to a party. When the starting-pistol fired, I was off like a bullet
through the gates, down the street, into Brasenose Wood, and
up the long flank of Shotover Hill. I knew every tree, every turn
in the path. Brambles that would snare strangers bent aside for
me. A friendly wind was at my back. I hadn't thought of poetry
for weeks, but now it came pouring into my head – a torrent of
Shakespeare (Henry V before Agincourt), Siegfried Sassoon:

> And I was filled with such delight,
> As prisoned birds must find in freedom,
> Winging wildly across the white
> Orchards and dark-green fields; on – on – and out of sight.

Before I reached the top of Shotover, the other runners were out
of sight and offered no challenge as I pounded past 'Shotover
Edge', down the familiar hill, and back through the barrack gates.

After a weekend's leave, the October intake (less an Elim
Pentecostal) was posted to the Light Infantry Brigade depot at
Strensall in Yorkshire, there to have any remaining dimples
ironed out and a uniform gloss applied. In early December, the
members of a Leader Platoon were dispatched to a War Office
Selection Board. This, in its wisdom, detected sufficient 'leader-
ship qualities' in most of us to warrant a posting to Eaton Hall
Officer Cadet School outside Chester.

We celebrated the arrival of those travel warrants with a

merry-go-round of Christmas dances in the arms of our Angelas, and then went back to arms drill of a less congenial kind. It was hard work learning how to be officers and gentlemen – and not immediately rewarding to poets – but in a few months we had a grasp of the essentials and, on 28 May, took our places in a Passing Out Parade under the eye of Princess Margaret. Unfortunately, when she came forward to inspect our burnished ranks, she passed under *our* eyes and few of us saw so much as the tip of her hat.

I caught a train to Oxford next day with a hangover and a Commission from her sister, **Elizabeth the Second** *by the Grace of God of the United Kingdom of Great Britain and Northern Ireland and of Her other Realms and Territories Queen, Head of the Commonwealth, Defender of the Faith.*

I wasn't altogether happy with the substitution of *Commonwealth* for *Imperium* and, indeed, would have preferred Her Majesty to have addressed me in Latin, but I was mollified by the terms of her address: '*To Our Trusty and well beloved Jon Howie Stallworthy Greeting! We, reposing especial Trust and Confidence in your Loyalty, Courage, and good Conduct, do by these Presents Constitute and Appoint you to be an Officer in our Land Forces from the Twenty ninth day of May 1954.*'

I was appointed Second Lieutenant in the Oxfordshire and Buckinghamshire Light Infantry; seconded to the 5th Battalion of the Nigeria Regiment of the Royal West African Frontier Force; and granted a month's embarkation leave in which to buy a dashing uniform, dance with Angela, enjoy strawberries and Sauterne and, in between, read poetry in the garden.

On my last afternoon in England, I took myself to *The Seekers*, a bad film in which hordes of Technicolor Maoris introduce a British sailor (Jack Hawkins) to life and death in the New Zealand bush. Thus prepared for the White Man's Grave, I climbed aboard a four-engined York with four other centurions seconded to Nigerian Legions: three Johns and Julian of the ill-matched boots. Our flight-path over the Mediterranean crossed

Officers' *giddah*

the *Orion*'s sealed wake, as we headed for Tripoli, the darkened Sahara, and points south. At Lagos we parted company: two Johns and Julian flying to Northern Nigeria; the third John and I squeezing ourselves and six suitcases into a jeep already containing another subaltern, a driver, a spare tyre, and a petrol can. If we hadn't been so tightly packed, we would probably have been thrown out as the driver, Hyacinth, hurled us down the 120 miles to Ibadan.

Arriving in the dripping dark of the rainy season, the newcomers were shown to what was to be our home for more than a year, a spacious bungalow, or *giddah*, with a high-pitched corrugated-iron roof projecting on three sides over a broad veranda. I was lucky in my housemate. John Hare and I had been friends at Eaton Hall and would share our *giddah* in high-spirited harmony unruffled even on hungover mornings or nights when one put a dead mamba in the other's bed.

We shared it, by day, with our 'boys' – Mussel Fort Lamy and

Mamu Basa – whose job was to keep it and us tidy; and we shared it, by night, with squadrons of mosquitoes and columns of ants, who would have emptied our veins and eaten us in our beds but for mosquito-nets and tobacco tins filled with kerosene in which our bed-legs stood

Our first visitors, apart from these, were a besieging force of traders, shoe-makers, and tailors – from one of whom we each ordered a white monkey-jacket and evening trousers, two pairs of white shorts, two pairs of khaki ones, and two khaki shirts. These cost £5 8s 6d of the £44 clothes allowance granted us by the Queen.

We got up at 6.30 every morning, pulled on a starched khaki shirt and shorts, buckled our Sam Browne belts, adjusted slouch hats with their black and green hackles, mounted our bikes, and set off down the road to Letmauk Barracks. The camp (as I always thought of it) was flanked by a single railway track. This was guarded by a sentry, whose bone-shaking rifle-salute had to be returned – a perilous moment for cyclists, who needed both hands to navigate the potholes. The camp buildings, all white-washed single-storey and roofed with corrugated iron, were grouped around a grassy area the size and shape of a rugger pitch edged with tall palm trees.

I had been assigned to D Company, having made the acquaintance of its National Service company commander in Tosswill's English Club and various rugger scrums at Rugby. The company office stood at the far end of the green rectangle, and to reach it I had to thread my way between dusky toddlers, dogs, and mangy chickens. To the left lay the company 'lines', home to the soldiers and their families. At that hour of the day, the women – many with babies on their backs – were outside their front doors, cutting up meat and yams for the morning *chop*. Reaching the company office at 7 o'clock, I would hand my bike to one of the guards and, with as much dignity as I could muster, mount the three steps to the green door.

That July, almost three-quarters of the company's 120 soldiers were on leave, so there was little for its officers to do. For my first few days, I read Somerset Maugham's short stories until, at 9 o'clock, it was time to reclaim my bike and ride back – past our *giddah* – to breakfast in the Officers' Mess. There, at a long table in a white room, we were waited on by barefooted mess-boys with scarlet cummerbunds and fezes. If a scorpion entered the mess, one of them would drop a linen napkin over it (to depress the sting) and stamp on it. No one was ever stung. By 9.45, we would be back in the company office, on the parade ground in the middle of the green rectangle, or on the rifle-range. We lunched at 1 o'clock, took a siesta, and then played games: at that season, squash with another officer, soccer or hockey with the soldiers.

These were drawn from Nigeria's three main tribes. Most of the riflemen were Hausas from the north; most of the clerks, cooks, drivers, storemen, and wireless operators either Ibos from the south-east or Yorubas from the south-west. Their pay, living conditions, and terms of service were good – better, relatively, than those of their British counterparts – and they were proud to be soldiers. The veterans had served in the Burma campaign of the Second World War, alarming the Japanese with their preference for cold steel. I was introduced to this when my houseboy, Mussel, quarrelled with another soldier over a woman. They took their machetes to each other, but when I visited them in hospital – one with an all-but-severed arm, the other with a cloven skull – they were in adjacent beds, roaring with laughter. Nigerian soldiers in the 1950s laughed a great deal, among themselves and with and at the British officers training them for their country's Independence (proposed for 1956, but deferred till 1960). I liked their generosity, good humour, openness, and warmth, and I think they liked me; my platoon sergeant, six-foot-two Umoru Lai (a soldier before I was born), treating me with the amused respect that a British miner might show a grammar-schoolboy son.

The problem of communications between officers and men –

Company 'lines'

lways an issue for imperial armies – was solved by the Romans
with characteristic efficiency: they simply taught their foreign
evies Latin. In the armies of the Russian Tsars, by contrast, the
non-commissioned officers often had to act as interpreters
between French-speaking officers and men speaking one of the
many languages of the Russian Empire. If the NCOs were
killed, officers and men could not communicate. The situation
in the Royal West African Frontier Force was closer to the
Roman model than the Russian, but the Queen's legions were
less efficient in this respect than Caesar's. Our levies were all volunteers, and all – Ibos, Hausas, and Yorubas – had a basic
qualification in 'English', but pidgin English, as taught in schools
or picked up afterwards. Pidgin is a written as well as spoken
language with its own rich vein of poetry, as revealed in the
glorious translation of the first chapter of *Genesis* beginning:

For the fors time nothing been dey only de Lawd na him dey; An
de Lawd He don go work hard for make a dis t'ing dem dey call
Earth. For six day de Lawd He work and He done make all t'ing –
everyt'ing He go put for Earth. Plenty beef, plenty cassava, plenty

banana, plenty yam, plenty guinea-corn, plenty mango, plenty groundnut – everyt'ing. An for de wata He put plenty fish, and for de air He put plenty kind bird.

After six day de Lawd He don go sleep. An' when He sleep plenty palaver start for dis place wey dem dey call Heaven. Dis heaven be place where we go live after we don die if we no do so-so bad for dis earth. De angeli dem live for Heaven an' play banjo an get plenty fine chop an' plenty palm wine.

Incoming National Service officers soon picked up a bastard form of pidgin (hence, two removes from standard English), adulterated with words and phrases from their soldiers' first languages. So, in the morning's disciplinary ritual known as Company Orders, a malefactor might be sentenced by a British officer to 'Three days *gwale gwale*' (Hausa for 'confined to barracks'). In more benevolent vein, telling someone not to worry, one could choose between pidgin, 'Maker no worree', or Hausa, '*Bar comi*'. In general, therefore, officers and men understood each other well enough, but on the football field there were misunderstandings in the goal mouth that made me wonder how well we would communicate in the cannon's mouth.

★

At the day's end, an officer would change out of games clothes into 'mess kit' – white monkey-jacket and trousers, scarlet cummerbund, 'George' boots, regimental cap – and walk over to the mess for supper. Afterwards, one might look in at the European Club, which was depressingly like the Chandrapore Club in Forster's *Passage to India*, or walk round Sabo market which was much more fun, especially on Friday nights when the soldiers had been paid. The traders, men and women, sat cross-legged on the ground with the flame of an oil-lamp lighting their wares. We seemed to walk through fallen galaxies, usually towards the blaze of a bonfire and the beat of drums. In the circle of firelight, a soldier inspirationally drunk on palm wine would be dancing, barefoot, miraculously in time to the intricate rhythms of an invisible orchestra of hands.

Some evenings we went to the open-air cinema, where the film always broke at moments of high drama, and where the door marked 'Ladies' (to the left of the screen) and that marked 'Gentlemen' (to the right) each opened into a corridor that led back to the same porcelain throne. There were also Cinema Nights in the mess, to which one could bring guests. I can't remember the film of the first I went to, but I remember one of the guests: a young woman in a white blouse. I didn't hear her name and wondered afterwards why I should remember her blouse.

Walking back to my *giddah* that night, for the first time I noticed the night train and remembered Kipling's in the Karroo:

> . . . we feel the far track humming,
> And we see her headlight plain,
> And we gather and wait her coming –
> The wonderful north-bound train.

Every night, from then on, I would listen for the triumphant hoot as it crested the hill, and watch for the glow of the great headlamp sweeping ahead of the cow-catcher. I came to love the rumble of its wheels, their clatter over the level-crossing and receding rumble into darkness and silence. The train became a friend. Also, in some obscure way, I associated it with the future. My mother had always said that each of her years was better than the last and, in the 1950s, I would have said the same of mine. The train spoke of the future and the future was a friend.

★

Every night, one of our number was *not* in white but khaki. This was the Orderly Officer and his duties were often surprising. The first time I was called out – buckling on the Orderly Officer's sword, and worried lest it catch in the spokes of my bike

123

– it was to bury a baby stillborn to the wife of a soldier then serving in Lagos. A three-ton truck was sent to collect a three-pound corpse that the relatives said should be buried in the 'bush' behind the lines. What about a coffin? And a service? No need for either, said the relatives, but I insisted on a coffin. The best they could find was a box stencilled GORDON'S GIN and, as a grumbling uncle wielded his spade, lines from *The Dragon Book of Verse* came incongruously to mind:

> We buried him darkly at dead of night,
> The sods with our bayonets turning;
> By the struggling moonbeam's misty light,
> And the lantern dimly burning.

On another occasion, I was called to the 'phone in the small hours to hear the crisp voice of the Colonel's wife saying that a police inspector had rung to report a 5 NR officer drunk and disorderly in the police station; and, she added, it didn't seem worth waking the Colonel, did it? I raced down to the station to find an Ibo subaltern, newly arrived from Sandhurst, trying to pick a fight with a Yoruba police inspector. My appeals to reason failing, I whispered to my colleague that if he didn't climb into my truck in two minutes, I would ask its driver to *throw* him in. He could see the driver was a large Yoruba and, cursing, climbed aboard. This and other such disruptions of what the Colonel called his 'family' should have alerted us to the troubles ahead but I know of no evidence that they did.

★

The Regiment was fortunate in its Colonel and its Colonel's wife: he, small and mild; she, large and martial; both of them generous and good-hearted. They shared a passion for polo which she played while he watched.

Neither John Hare nor I had ever seen the game before but within weeks of arriving in Ibadan, I was telling my parents:

John and I are now thinking of sharing the cost of a £20 roan, which besides being a good, quiet but skilful polo pony is one of the fastest racers in the district. There is an excellent *doki*-boy, who will exercise and generally tend him for £1 per month: food costs about another £1, all of which we would share, John having it for the months I am at Lagos, and I having it during his months on detachment and during his mortar-course. . . . I don't think the cost is too bad when you are drawing £28 a month, only about £10 being taken by the mess bill.

I'm afraid I told a lie when I said this *doki*, Kadilla, was 'quiet'. I neglected to say he was a stallion and dangerous at both ends: mounting him, one risked being bitten in the bottom or kicked in the crotch but, once mounted, he was a joy to ride. He came second in the Polo Scurry (a race for polo ponies) at the Ibadan Races that August and, early in September, became ours. With Kadilla came his *doki*-boy, a salaried soldier called Aly Lai, who loved him dearly and treated him tenderly, even on the rare occasions when he was himself bitten or kicked.

Every evening, a burnished Kadilla would be saddled and waiting for John or me to take him out. The first time it was my turn, I rode him up to the regimental polo ground where a game was in progress. As I approached, the white ball shot out of a mêlée with two riders in pursuit – a large officer and a small woman. Heeling to the left, like a yacht in the wind, she rode him off the path of the ball, then heeling to the right, gave her polo-stick a wristy flick. There was a sharp crack and the ball flew between the goal posts.

'Who's that?' I asked a bystander.

'Hazel,' he said, 'Hazel Munro. Rides like a Cossack.'

Only then did I recognize her as the wearer of the white blouse. She was in her late twenties, a recently arrived physiotherapist at Ibadan's Jericho Hospital and, I soon discovered, a principal cause of the popularity of polo among officers of the Regiment.

I had played hockey for Southern Nigeria, but couldn't hit a

Aly Lai and Kadilla

polo ball with the stick lent me by the Colonel's wife. Neither John nor I could afford a new stick of our own, so we devised a plan. Kadilla must win us prize-money in the October Races, and the best chance of that would be if he had a Cossack in the saddle. We put it to Hazel as a business proposition: she would win us the money for polo-sticks, and we would buy her dinner with any surplus. Her smile was like the headlamp of the night train, dazzling.

'All *right!*' she said.

John and I were at the finishing post, shouting ourselves hoarse, as she and Kadilla flashed past second in the Polo Scurry. Over supper, we asked ourselves who should ride him in the November Races, and spun a coin. I won. We increased Kadilla's ration of corn and every evening exercised him on the race-track.

I was Orderly Officer on the Saturday of the Races. Looking in at Kadilla's stable before dawn, I found him pawing the floor and tossing his head in challenging fashion. As I counted rifles in the armoury and inspected cookhouses, my mind was on a *doki*'s diet: had he had enough corn? Should I have galloped him last night? I had a minimal lunch myself and, having found a friend to stand in as Orderly Officer, was soon in the saddling enclosure, collecting a numbered saddle-cloth and pulling on a crimson shirt. The mounting bugle sounded, girths and stirrups were checked, and up we went, first to walk round the paddock, its white rail topped with a hedgerow of faces. As we passed, one shouted (in a strong Scottish accent): 'Ah've tain shelling on yew. Ah hope its safe. Yew luke fain at any rate.' I just had time to say that I didn't *feel* fain before the second bugle sounded and the colourful cavalcade moved out on to the track.

Kadilla by now was passaging, tossing his head, and working himself into a fine frenzy. I was worried that, with only a light racing-bit and no curb chain to restrain him, he might bolt, but we reached the start safely. I had drawn number two, of twelve. Inside me on the rails was the favourite, Mercury, a racehorse proper, and already twice a winner that afternoon. We came forward in line and the flag dropped. Supe, number five, was first away and cut in to take the rails. At the second bend, Kadilla was third, with Venus – another racehorse – half a length up on the outside. There was no sign of Mercury or two others with short odds.

As we thundered into the home stretch, Supe and Venus fell away, broken by the rising ground, and suddenly there was no more grit flicking my face. Two hundred yards to go . . . a hundred and fifty . . . and then, at my elbow, appeared Mercury's white star. I heard his jockey shouting and shouted myself. I gave Kadilla a touch of the whip – not as a spur but a signal – and the star fell back, only to advance again as Mercury also felt the whip. His black neck crept past us. One minute, the finishing post was far ahead, the next, far behind. And, for the fifth time in a row, Kadilla had come second. Back in the enclosure, Aly Lai was kissing him on the nose when up jumped the Scotsman, saying 'Ah don't mind lusing ma tain shelling!'

Some hours later, I was celebrating at the club when my torpid conscience roused itself to remind me I had to inspect the Battalion night guard – in five minutes. I had no time to change into uniform, so Hazel drove me into camp and I turned out the guard in my suit and regimental tie. As I was inspecting them, a familiar jungle-green Landrover drew up in the compound and I could hear the Colonel and his second-in-command talking. Somehow they didn't see me in their headlights, and I was able to dismiss the guard and escape undetected in Hazel's getaway car.

If this suggests a cavalier attitude towards my military duties, I like to think it was corrected by Pat Cunningham, who took command of D Company on my Rugbeian friend's return to England. Pat was 20, said to be the youngest captain in the British Army and, in every sense, a regular soldier. I thought of him as Wordsworth's 'happy Warrior . . . he/ That every man in arms should wish to be'. Well over six foot, he had the advantage of looking like Errol Flynn but, far from being a self-regarding swashbuckler, directed his energies and intelligence to the welfare of his men: black and white, they would have followed him to hell and back.

Pat Cunningham

Fortunately, we were only required to follow him to French Dahomey and back.

*

The occasion for this was the Company Trek, a training exercise valuable not for what it taught us about fighting together so much as living together; the latter is a necessary preliminary to the former.

It began at 3 a.m. on 1 December, with three officers and fifty-eight men 'present and correct' outside the company office. When, towards dawn on the road south out of Ibadan, the company transport roared past the column in a blaze of lights, Pat Cunningham was probably the only man not longing for a lift. As the sun came up and the shirts began to darken with sweat, he found the track into the bush he had been looking for,

D Company on trek

and we turned into the green tunnel that would bring us – after seventeen miles on the march – to our first camp. Platoon positions had been cleared by the machetes of the advance guard, carried in the trucks with the cooks, who had their fires crackling and tea brewed.

Eating and sleeping side by side in this and other clearings, we came to know each other better: who grumbled, who laughed, who was generous, who was greedy. Following Pat's example, we began to help each other – and enjoy each other – more. Cigarettes and jokes were shared, waterbottles passed from hand to hand. We would break camp before sunrise and set off through the bush, often in single file, with a pearly mist between us and the tree-tops. Some mornings, our route followed a road, and for the first hour or so we would march in darkness and silence. Then from one end of the column would come a shout, to be taken up like an echo by a voice at the other end, and the singing would begin. They sang the sort of songs I would expect from fishermen, casting and drawing in their nets on the coasts of Africa; songs like sea shanties, but enlivened with a weird hop, step and jump rhythm I had come to associate with the inland tribes. Rising and falling, the waves of sound rolled backwards and forwards down the swaying column. From Maitumbi Zuru the high-pitched solo lead would be passed to Garba Gombe and bounce on like a ball to be caught and thrown back by Mallam Lai . . .

Marching and singing, we passed through Abeokuta and Awlawrunda. At Aiyetoro, we were advised to pay our respects to 'the King', and crossing the courtyard of his palace, three officers of the Queen were ushered into a throne room where a coloured photograph of Her Majesty hung beside an elaborately carved wooden monkey. *His* Majesty then entered, fanning himself with an embroidered fly-switch, and courtesies were exchanged. Captain Cunningham requested a guide for the next day's march through the bush to Mekkaw. This was granted and we withdrew. At Mekkaw, we were received by another king who, not to be outshone by our uniforms, retired to robe himself in yet greater splendour and re-entered with a gold chain and mitre-like crown of scarlet and white beadwork. Next day, he very graciously sent us a present of yams. Ruefully aware that imperial bounty was not what it had been, we could only reciprocate with a tin of coffee and two packets of biscuits.

Mekkaw was a frontier town, but the frontier itself lay some miles to the west and, since the enforcing of frontiers was our special responsibility, we thought we should inspect it. Giving the legion a rest-day, the centurions set off in the Landrover down the long straight road. Soon a *tricolore* came in sight, and our nostrils twitched to a rich scent that we couldn't identify – until, as the bamboo barrier lifted to let us through into Dahomey, we saw the demijohns of wine, the crowd at the *Douanes* smoking Gauloises. We drove on to the village of Ketu and in the market bought 325-franc flagons of *Grand Vin*

Crossing the Awyan

Muscadin from a Dahomeyan speaking perfect French. Returning more sedately, lest the potholes crack our precious cargo, I noticed that this was not a problem beyond the bamboo barrier. Ahead of us stretched the Roman road and (at first) sober reflections on the priorities of empire: roads and pidgin English versus *Grand Vin Muscadin* and perfect French.

At Mekkaw, the legion turned for home, taking a northerly route that brought us after two days' march to the bank of the River Awyan. Grey and fast-flowing, this reminded me of the question put to almost every would-be officer at his War Office Selection Board: 'How would you get your men across a river that . . . [only the details differed]?' Pat Cunningham knew the answer: you call for volunteers to swim across and find a boat.

Usika Dila and Jalengo stepped forward: 'This like my country, sah. I savvy swim.' And swim they did, to the accompaniment of cheers from the non-swimmers and those who wanted to keep their feet dry. On the far bank, they found a dug-out canoe and a long pole with which Jalengo punted it

back. Six times it crossed and recrossed the river with its complement of soldiers and, bringing up the rear, I remembered a
Maori war canoe at the Dragon School Rag Regatta.

Moving on from the dense bush of the river basin, we
climbed to a yellow plain of 'orchard bush' out of which, six or
seven miles ahead, rose a line of sudden blue hills. On one of
these we camped and, next day, climbed into more mountainous country – where we practised ambush and night patrols –
before descending to the Oloko-Meji forest reserve. Here we
found a Government Rest House with a game-book that
recorded a fifty-pound perch caught in the nearby river,
together with an occasional crocodile; and from the bush,
duiker, antelope, and red river-hog. The Colonel joined us for
our last lantern-lit supper and, the following day, we marched
the twenty-nine miles back to Ibadan in five and a half hours. It
was four in the morning when we reached the polo field at the
edge of the camp, and the men – determined that no one should
miss their homecoming – broke into song again. Wives and children poured out of the 'lines' to meet them. On the parade
ground, Pat congratulated his legion on its 210-mile march,
Sergeant-Major Dauda shouted '*Comp'ny Dis-miss!*', and we all
went home to bed.

★

I woke to a pleasant surprise. Among the Christmas cards and
Sunday letters from Shotover Edge awaiting my return was an
invitation to the Ibadan University Christmas Eve ball – from the
beautiful Cossack. I knew she'd had a bad fall from a horse while
I was away. John Hare said the invitation showed her brain had
been affected, but she certainly looked well on the night. At the
supper table, my place-card read 'Mr Munro', a misunder-
standing it would by then have been more embarrassing to
correct than to accept, so accept it we did. It was a role I was
happy to play and, indeed, would have been happy to play on

after the last waltz, had I not been led – very gently – to understand that my promotion was temporary, acting, and carried no privileges.

I had read *Sons and Lovers* on trek and was full of Lawrentian longings, which I cooled over Christmas in a swimming pool shadowed by laden branches of a grapefruit tree. Soon, I was told, I would have better swimming – on the beaches of Lagos, where D Company was to be 'on detachment' for three and a half months from the end of February. The prospect didn't please me. I should have preferred to remain, like Tantalus in *his* pool, hungering for fruit that was always out of reach.

The end of February arrived with six trucks to be loaded with soldiers, *matas*, *pikins*, bedrolls, and cooking pots. I was in charge of the convoy and, halting it once an hour to let everyone stretch their legs, was driven to desperation by the difficulty of herding them back again. But finally it was done and, having supervised their installation in the Dodan barracks, I was heading for a lonely weekend in the Officers' Mess when a familiar Opel Rekord drew up. Hazel and two other friends had come to test the Lagos beaches.

A military launch carried us across Lagos Harbour to the white-hot sands of Tarquah Bay, where from a palm tree's shade we watched a line of fishermen, waist-deep in the surf, swinging and casting their nets, then plunged into the surf ourselves. The following day, a Sunday, we went back with a picnic and 'tired the sun with talking', ourselves with swimming, until it was time for the last launch to unzip the harbour's watered silk. 'Another weekend,' we said, 'we'll try Lighthouse Beach.'

On the Monday night, I was Orderly Officer with guards to turn out at various points around the city. Our barracks overlooked the lagoon, and for half a mile my route followed the waterfront. I saw the fishermen's firefly lanterns flare and vanish, the tankers riding at anchor on their reflected lights, each like a swinging candelabrum. There was a ripe moon. I thought of the grapefruit over the swimming pool in Ibadan, and I thought of

Hazel with (I hoped) only her cat, Tweed, to keep her company – though, no doubt, there would be 'the usual suspects' competing for that honour. Before I was back in barracks, I was talking to her in my head:

Somewhere between February and March 1955

> Dear Hazel,
>   February goes home
> On tides of darkness, a dim foam
> Lapping in light the seaward moon:
> And hourlong over the lagoon
> The Lagos lights burn old.
>   Tonight
> I hold the castle – Hell's delight –
> Do not believe them who would say;
> '*Les lieutenants sont toujours gais –*'
> But glass in left hand, pen in right,
> Intending to outwear the night
> I put behind me place and time,
> And hopeful-hearted, turn to rhyme
> To set my inhibitions free,
> And you to keep me company.
>
> Tarquah's unsentimental tides
> Devour our footprints, darkness hides
> Subaltern's cove and mermaid's lair:
> Yet fade they not, though from my chair
> The bounds of hearing do not reach
> To wind and surf on Lighthouse Beach.
> And for those days that take this tide
> I thank you, that they now abide
> With other days and hours well-spent,
> In the far uplands of content.
>
> All things to Sleep's wide kingdom come:
> You too – or is not Tweedle dumb;
> Or at your louvers, say, is Rudi

Exchanging shots with Alan Frudey?
And are complaints heard round the site
That 'baby cannot sleep at night
Without the troops' familiar row'?

God! to be in Ibadan now
Where streets at night are cool and still,
And lights along the whale-backed hill
Throw back the brilliance of the stars.
Hushed there the din of day, and cars
Like moonlit cattle shadow-graze,
And dream of oil in alleyways.

Yet beats a pulse there; if you go
Through Sabo on a path I know
Where wick-lamps gilding hand and eye
An earthly constellation lie,
A drum-loud kingdom will you find
Where cripples caper, and the blind
Unroll their livid eyes to chase
The King of Diamonds and the Ace.

Tell me, does Kadilla's ghost
Play havoc with the stallion host,
And Aly Lai when day wears dim,
Hear you the homing shout of him? . . .

But you are sleeping: sleep you sound
The spent moon and the starlight round,
Dreaming of Tarquah, whose pale sands
Warm wonderfully idle hands . . .
Though dreams and vigils fade again,
Remember, the long sands remain.
Damn!
          Duty calls: the guards await
And Dawn comes early to the gate.
Reveille, raking soon the skies,
Will shake the matchsticks from my eyes.
My nib crawls slow, the glass is dry –

So for a little while 'goodbye',
'*A bientôt le revoir, mignonne*':
Regards to all –
                    and you?
                        love –
                            Jon.

P.S. Oh yes,
                    Kadilla too
Sends his most fond regards to you;
And will you mark a further score
Of notches on his stable door?

Five minutes on . . .
                        I cannot cope
With this most stubborn envelope.
What made you choose a home address
Without ONE rhyme, I cannot guess.
Be thankful then I did not write
In my frustration, as I might –

            Miss H. Munro,
            The one you know
        Who theraps in the Jericho;
            Whose favours gladden
            Madden or sadden
                Every lad'n
                IBADAN.

Apprentice poets have to learn not to waste words, and behind
this letter I can hear – recycled and condensed – another one,
written home at the end of January, describing a midnight stroll
in the Sabo quarter of Ibadan:

It might have been the kingdom of the beggars out of *The Arabian
Nights*. On every side, the darkness was kept at bay by a twinkling
sea of tiny wick lanterns, and behind each one, their scarred faces
falling constantly through light to shadow, crouched the sellers of
bread and dried fish, kola nuts and cassava, silks and slippers, tinned

food and palm wine. Filth unlimited; the deceptively sweet stench of the great unwashed; colour, in the contrast between light and darkness, rags and cloths more brilliant than the rainbow, almost too dazzling for sight. Here I felt, during the hours of darkness, the halt and the maimed cast aside their crutches; the paralyzed beggar forgot his pitch in the shade of the flame tree, in the glory of dancing to the frenzied drumming and shaking and bowing of the music makers. The blind received their sight, and squatting shoulder to shoulder on the round grass mats, dealt out greasy cards and pulled in precious pennies and sixpences with claw-like fingers. Never have I seen cards so dextrously shuffled, flicked – half the pack from each hand – into a central pile.

My epistolary *jeu d'esprit* also owes something of its structure and tone to Rupert Brooke's 'The Old Vicarage, Grantchester', but has perhaps more of its own voice than earlier poems from the same pen.

A fortnight later, Hazel again drove down to Lagos and, taking the launch to Tarquah Bay, we crossed to Lighthouse Beach. It was all that we had hoped, a surf-pounded strip of white sand stretching almost uninterrupted from Lagos to Accra.

The following week I was back in Ibadan, playing in a game of polo that suddenly caught fire. At half-time, the Colonel jumped into his Landrover, drove the two miles to his second-in-command's *giddah*, and shouted: 'Come and see the polo! They're going like bats out of hell!' Hazel and I were on different sides and, in the second half, as we converged on a speeding ball (which we both missed), her whirling stick caught me under the chin. The wound was neither deep nor painful; quite the reverse, the shock seemed to carry a sexual voltage. 'First blood to you,' I said, and her eyes flashed as if she felt the current too.

She had been riding Groucho, a newly acquired racehorse she hoped would recoup the £30 he had cost her. He was entered for the Lagos Races in April. On the day – a day when I rode Kadilla to a poor fifth in the Polo Scurry – Groucho (and a professional African jockey) won three races and £360 pounds.

Hazel and *Captain Rose*

That evening, Hazel was the toast of the Ikoyi Club, where we danced until midnight and then, it seemed simultaneously, thought of a better way of spending the rest of the night. Driving down to the harbour, we found a fisherman prepared to ferry us over the harbour for a few pounds. And so, for the first time, I dropped my army haversack and Hazel her leather beach-bag in the stern of the *Captain Rose*, and climbed aboard. Sitting on the bow thwart, the fisherman dug his paddle into the darkness and produced a miracle – a phosphorescent flash, between the steady brilliance of the stars and the swinging candelabra of the ships. When we were clear of the land, he hoisted a lug-sail of patchworked flour sacks and, forty-five minutes later, the *Captain Rose* hissed to a halt in the sand of Tarquah Bay. Leaving the fisherman to sleep, we walked hand in hand to Lighthouse Beach and found it magically transformed. The sand was warm velvet and the lighthouse was at work, every eight seconds, swinging its great beam over our heads. Even the surf was different: a white comb drawn through the darkness. Entering the water, we too were transfigured, tattooed with phosphorescence.

At last, tired of swimming and surfing, we stretched out on warm velvet, fed each other sections of tangerine, and began to talk as we hadn't talked before. She told me she had been in love with a stylish older man, who used to send her bunches of red roses until, one day, a bunch came with a card saying he had married someone else. Devastated, she had immediately applied for jobs overseas and arrived in Ibadan shortly before me.

'Providential!' I said.

'Perhaps.' And on that provisional note we fell asleep, with a thermos of cooling coffee like Tristram's sword between us.

It was the first time I had woken with a woman beside me, and I was filled with wonder at her presence, her small-breasted, slim-hipped beauty. Did I think – or was it afterwards I thought – of Keats's Porphyro gazing at the sleeping Madeline, and the outcome of the ceremonies of St Agnes Eve?

> Into her dream he melted, as the rose
> Blendeth its odour with the violet, –
> Solution sweet . . .

Certainly, that was the solution I had in mind, as Hazel woke with a different solution. She smiled and said: '*Good* morning. Give me a kiss – and then some cold coffee.'

Another weekend, we found another paradisal beach, at Badagry, sixty miles of sand track from Lagos, and camped in a rest-house. This had a cheerful caretaker, who cut wood for the stove, primed the kerosene fridge, and went marketing for us. Our two days began at 6.30 when, with the palms and flame-trees colourless against the silver lagoon in front of the house, I paddled a canoe to the sand-bar on its further side. A quarter of an hour's walk through a grove of towering palms brought us to the beach. This was too steep for surf-boarding but wonderful for swimming. It was also deserted, except for one evening when the families of fishermen poured out from the village to greet the return of a nine-man canoe. The steersman was standing at its knife-like stern, his crew rowing in perfect unison. They paused behind the outer surf, then shot forward with it, striking faster to catch the second line, and raced in. We ran down the sand with the whooping families and helped haul the canoe up the beach. Its catch included a hammer-head shark.

In the cool of the evening, I paddled across the lagoon – past inshore fishermen swinging their lariat-like nets – back to a kerosene lantern, a roaring stove, supper with Hazel and (this was the catch) a friend. If Eden had to have a third party, I decided, let it be the serpent.

★

Some months before, I had acknowledged the sea-change in my affections with a sonnet that moved, once again, to the swing of the sea. I called it 'High Tide':

> Once upon a dancing time, when curtained round,
> Low rooms awash with music learnt the flow
> Of shifting feet and satin's undertow,

In a foam of light and laughter I was drowned.
You, in the doorway, made the dancers grow
Remote as the stiff paintings on the wall.
The clock stood speechless: fingers ceased to fall
Tumultuous on pied keys.

                                    I thought to go
For my part of forever, seeing you –
As in that instant when things known were strange –
Beyond believing beautiful. But slow
And strong the long tides lift anew;
Laughter and light return; the dancers change
With this illusion of a year ago.

The poem makes its bow to Angela at the end of our dance. Technically, too, it represents a departure. I had attempted any number of Shakespearean sonnets before, but never a Petrarchan one, which calls for a structural divide (known as 'the turn') between an opening statement and a closing counter-statement. The tide turns later than it should in my poem, and the rhyme-scheme of the first eight lines is imperfect (*abba, bccb*, rather than *abba, abba*), but at least my structural instinct was sound.

Back from Badagry, I sat down to address another lady in another sonnet, this time a Shakespearean one, the most traditional of all forms of love poem:

Riding the waves white-saddled under the moon,
I have put on their glory, in their strength
Forgotten my light limbs; and come at length
Where the spent waters die along the dune.
There wave-worn kneeling, I would watch awhile
The sickle bend of sand on sky, and one
Tiara'd with the antique stars. I run
Still in my dreams that last slope to your smile.
So when at length, its ermine drawn behind,
Some wave shall leave me on Elysian sand,
I would climb no more weary where you stand;

> Feel your blown hair across my face, and find –
> From seas secure, withdrawn from earth's alarms –
> All heaven about me, breathless in your arms.

There is no 'turn' here, only a *return* to a shared world of 'riding
. . . sand on sky . . . your blown hair across my face'; and no
counter-statement, only a single statement climbing through its
three quatrains from sea to sand to heaven. But again the language is antiquated and there are technical flaws: again, the
rhyme-scheme of the quatrains is imperfect (*abba, cddc, effe*,
rather than *abab, cdcd, efef*). It's a pity, too, about the first line of
the concluding couplet. I should have worked harder on that.

★

Hazel had entered Groucho for the June Races in Lagos, and
again he galloped home ahead of the field. This time he won
£120, bringing his gross earnings over recent months to £860.
His delighted owner was staying with the friend who had
accompanied us to Badagry, and together they prepared a celebratory supper. When my contribution – the champagne – was
finished and the candle burnt to its socket, Hazel offered to drive
me back to barracks. It was a velvet night with a full moon riding
low and golden over the lagoon.

'Let's go to the beach,' she said.

That seemed a better idea, but I had to be on parade – and
she on the road to Ibadan – at dawn. That didn't give us time to
get to Tarquah and back, so we drove to a nearer beach, Victoria.
In the far distance, some sort of ceremony was taking place at
the edge of the churning surf. We could see lights and hear
chanting.

'Know something?' I said.

'What?'

'We haven't got our bathing suits.'

'Nor we have, but never mind.'

We spread the rug and lay down.

'Perhaps they're honouring the moon.'

'What a good idea'.

I helped her off with her shirt. She helped me off with mine, and we peeled off the rest. Our bodies were mahogany, inlaid each with a broad band of ivory and a little triangle of ebony. We kissed each other's ivory and, with tender reverence, made our libations to the moon.

Later, she said: 'I think they must be right.'

'Who?'

'The people who say a woman always keeps her first lover warm in a corner of her heart.'

'What about a man?'

'I don't know about men.'

'I know about one man.'

'Tell me,' she said.

★

My days in Nigeria were numbered. I expected to be flown home in the last week of August, which left us twelve weekends. We didn't waste one. The rains were now back – 8.41 inches falling on Lagos in one 24-hour period – but were merciful at weekends: silver squalls filling culverts and ditches in a matter of minutes, then snatched aside like curtains to reveal our old friend the sun. He escorted the *Captain Rose* on numerous crossings to Tarquah Bay and, when D Company returned to Ibadan in late July, led the jingling posse of Sunday-morning riders. Waking in Hazel's bedroom, I might say (for I was just rediscovering the poems of John Donne):

> Busy old fool, unruly sun,
> Why dost thou thus
> Through windows and through curtains call on us?
> Must to thy motions lovers' seasons run?

But then I would remember it was Sunday and by 6.30 we had to be at so-and-so's house or such-and-such a point in the bush. We would tumble out of bed into our clothes and then the car. The *doki*-boys and their charges would be at the rendezvous first, or second only to the 'host' of the day, who would give us each a 'horse's neck' of brandy and ginger as we arrived. Then, swinging into the saddle, we set off down sandy tracks into the jungle, sometimes jumping a fallen tree or splashing through a stream. Kadilla pretended to dislike water, and there were days when much pawing of the bank and tossing of the head took place before, with a snort of disapproval, he would step in and canter through. One day, after these preliminaries, reaching the middle of an unusually broad stream, he stopped, gave a sigh, rolled over and wallowed. Mercifully, I slipped my feet out of the stirrups in time and suffered nothing worse than an undignified ducking. The 'kind old sun' dried me out before the ten-mile circuit ended at our host's *giddah* with bacon and eggs, more brandy and ginger, and gallons of coffee.

★

On weekdays, I was still ostensibly a soldier. My duties in Lagos had been largely ceremonial. I had flourished a sword in a Guard of Honour for a departing Governor-General, in another for his plumed successor, and in a thunderous Queen's Birthday Parade on Lagos racecourse. Returning to Ibadan, we returned to training. One Sunday in August I wrote home:

All my waking hours this week I have been supervising troops at their range-firing – at times a little boring – but topographically, such a pleasant change from Lagos. The range itself – a great, 400-yard swathe of green levelled from the crest of a hill, overlooks on one side the little white square of barracks, and on all others, palm-tree and bush, valley and hill for miles without number. When the rifles are silent, there is no sound save the wind in the clouds: the impression of height, depth, and space is remarkable. Even the train in that world is an event of interest. With its searchlight and cow-catcher in the best pioneer tradition, it crests the hill with an asthmatic toot of triumph that never fails to bring the soldiers' heads round from their targets. But then they are not really soldiers; for although they polish and drill and shoot, I feel they do it only to humour the mad white men from whom they draw their pay. I do not blame them, for never were soldiers so out of touch with war in its contemporary colours. The word tank means nothing to them and the only function they associate with an aeroplane is the bringing of mail up from Lagos. So until the next tribal war, in which alone would they be of use, they eat and sleep, dance, have children, and smile at the strange ways of mad white men.

When I said goodbye to them on 14 September (the gods having granted me three more golden weekends), it was with a warmth of affection in those sixty handshakes that some, I like to think, returned. My affection was tinged with sadness, in the knowledge that I should not hear from many – if, indeed, any – of them again. Few of those sixty hands could do more with a pen than write a name. In August 1955, my own pen wrote of 'the next tribal war' as a remote possibility without the shiver that accompanies the rewriting of those words forty years later.

★

On the evening of 15 September, I was 'dined out' of the mess and returned to the *giddah* to get ready for going Home. That was my excuse for not drinking till dawn. What I wanted to do first was write a letter that Hazel would receive when Flight #W2/70 was somewhere between Kano and Stanstead, but as I sat at the table – now stripped of its books and photographs – the word 'Home' tolled like a cracked bell in my head, and I felt a sadness I had never felt before. What was Home? If it was anywhere, it was the flat where I should be welcomed for the last time in an hour or so.

As I wrote my letter, the table began to vibrate. It was my old friend, the train, with its approaching rumble, the clatter of wheels apparently on the veranda, the light passing, the rumble passing, the vibration passing, and then there were only the crickets scratching the silence.

Midnight brought another vibration, another light, as Hazel drove up to take me home. When the 'Busy old fool, unruly sun' came to call on us, we hadn't slept. We kissed – not for the last time, we told each other. She went back to bed, burying her face in the pillow, and I walked from the door into the future, with tears streaming down my unsoldierly cheeks.

6

Public Performance

I READ LITTLE in Nigeria – Life being more important than
Literature – but had occasionally asked my mother to send me a
book from a Shotover bookshelf or from Blackwells. The last
such request, a second-hand copy of *Sweet's Anglo-Saxon Primer*
(recommended on a reading-list from Oxford), I opened on the
long flight home. It began with a definition:

> The oldest stage of English, from the earliest records (about A.D. 700)
> to soon after the Norman Conquest, is now generally called 'Old
> English', though the name 'Anglo-Saxon' is still often used. There
> were several dialects of Old English. This grammar deals only with
> the *West Saxon* dialect, the most important for the study of the lit-
> erature; and with the early form of it – that is, the language of about
> the time of King Alfred.

So far so good, but no further. I was soon floundering among
Sound-Changes: 'a knowledge of them is necessary for an
understanding of the grammar. The essentials only are set out
here.' The essentials were too much for me. Weak and Strong
Declensions were much too much for me. I turned to the smor-
gasbord of Anglo-Saxon texts at the back of the book: extracts
from the Old and New Testaments and from a translation of
Bede's Ecclesiastical History. There were no poems. I shuddered.
Anglo-Saxon was clearly a subject to be endured rather than

enjoyed. I closed the book – '*Sweets to the sweet, farewell*' – and opened another bottle of beer.

★

A confused fortnight later, however, *Sweet's Primer* and my spongebag were the only contents of my Nigerian luggage to be transferred to the case I carried into Magdalen.

I had put my name down for that college, two and a half years earlier, on the advice of a family friend who told me C.S. Lewis was the senior English Tutor there. Soon after I arrived, and before we had met (but perhaps my reputation had preceded me), he moved to Cambridge. I can't pretend I was seriously disappointed, and probably learned more from his successor, a young Shakespearean scholar called Emrys Jones, than I would have from the lordly Lewis who, it was said, would sometimes read the newspaper while a pupil read him his essay.

In October 1955, the college admitted six freshmen to read English. Initially this meant *Old* English, into the mysteries of which we were to be initiated by a distinguished medievalist, who already had a place in our family folklore. Jack Bennett was a gnomelike New Zealander and a friend of my father, who had recently delivered his first child. Jack was not present at the birth, and my father suggested to his wife, Gwyneth, that she ring him with the happy news.

'Oh, no,' she said, 'he's teaching.'

'But he'll want to come,' said her obstetrician.

'No.'

'Why ever not?'

'He wouldn't know *where* to come.'

'He doesn't know the Radcliffe Infirmary?'

'No. He only knows the bus-route between our house and Magdalen.'

'Then I'll get him,' said my father, who thereupon rang the distinguished medievalist. No sooner had he announced himself than his friend said: 'I'm afraid I can't talk now. I'm teaching.'

'I have to talk to you', said my father, 'because Gwyneth's just had a baby boy and I know you'll want to see them –'

'But I'm teaching.'

'Well, I suggest you stop, and meet me in the Lodge in fifteen minutes.' And before Jack could protest, my father put the phone down. He duly collected him, introduced him to his son, and returned him – radiantly confused – to college.

My father said Jack was unworldly, but that was wrong. He simply lived in a different world: that of the Middle Ages. Why should he take *The Times* when he had *The Anglo-Saxon Chronicle*, or buy a lawn-mower when he had a scythe?

Entering his college room, we entered his world.

'You may have asked yourselves why you need to know Old English.' We had. He told us that the answers to this question – and there were two – would soon be obvious to us. They were. First, that Old English is a principal ingredient of Modern English and, until we understood that, we couldn't fully understand our own language, our own literature. Second, that reading Old English would enable us to enjoy the first good prose, and the first great poems, in our literary inheritance. He told us we would have to master the principles of *Sweet's Primer* – largely on our own – by the end of our second term (when we would be examined); and that, in the meantime, he would take us through the texts.

This he did, starting with the poems, and in his mouth their 'dead' language came alive. I loved the specificity of a sword being an *ecg* (edge), a lord being a *hlaford* (a contraction of *hlaf-weard*, a loaf-guardian, a giver of bread). I could see why Hopkins had modelled his new 'sprung rhythm' on Old English metre, and why Pound had admired 'The Seafarer' enough to translate it.

Jack Bennett was a devout Roman Catholic. He read 'The Dream of the Rood' as a believer, and 'The Battle of Maldon' as a belated contemporary. I came to share his enthusiasm for both, particularly the anonymous warrior-poet's celebration of Byrhtnoth's last stand, encapsulated in his old retainer's last speech:

> *Byrhtwold mathelode,   bord hafenode,*
> *se waes eald geneat,   aesc acwhete,*
> *he ful baldlice   beornas laerde:*
> *'Hige sceal the heardra,   heorte the cenre,*
> *mod sceal the mara,   the ure maegen lytlath.*
> *Her lith ure ealdor   eall forheawen,*
> *god on greota;   a maeg gnornian*
> *se the nu fram this wigplegan   wendan thenceth.*
> *Ic eom frod feores: fram ic ne wille,*
> *ac ic me be healfe   minum hlaforde*
> *be swa leofan men   licgan thence.'**

But if this poem described an actual battle, who wrote it? If the Saxons fought to the last man, had the poet fled from the battle? 'Yes and no,' said our tutor. Poets of the heroic age were expected to take their place in the shield-wall. (As a front-row forward, I approved of that.) But if the *comitatus* was facing certain defeat, its poet was expected to retire and raise the elegy by which alone his companions' deeds would be remembered down the generations. So Aneirin, poet of 'The Gododdin', said he left the battle of Catraeth 'soaked in blood for my song's sake'.

All this was explained by Jack Bennett, the most gentle and peaceable of men who, by a strange irony, was required to introduce his freshmen not only to 'The Battle of Maldon' and *Beowulf*, but also to another martial epic, Virgil's *Aeneid*, on Books IV and VI of which we were also to be examined in our

---

* 'Birhtwold spoke, raised his shield – he was an old retainer – shook his ash-spear; full boldly he exhorted the men: "Purpose shall be the firmer, heart the keener, courage shall be the more, as our might lessens. Here lies our lord all hewn down, good man on ground. Ever may he lament who now thinks to turn from war-play. I am old of life; from here I will not turn, but by my lord's side, by the man I loved, I intend to lie."'

second term. After more than ten years in the foothills of Latin literature, finally I reached the mountains and there, as with Old English, alarm soon gave way to excitement. The story of Dido and Aeneas – his desertion, her death, his last glimpse of her in the Underworld – meant more to me at 20 than it would have earlier. I could now 'hear' the oceanic surge of the Latin and understand how the confluence of those warm tides with ice-cold Anglo-Saxon had produced the language that was now my element.

Introducing me to the composition of my 'word-hoard', which a writer should understand as a painter the composition of his pigments, Jack Bennett also introduced me to the dream of the long poem.

★

Hazel and I had been writing to each other since I had left Nigeria and, in November, returning to England on leave, she drove down to Oxford. It was a reunion about which we had fantasized together in Ibadan and Lagos, dreamt about separately since; a reunion both longed for and, at a deeper level, dreaded. And this was the day. Grey sky over grey stone, and the leaves falling. I had slept badly, woken early, and fidgeted around in a fever of impatience until, about mid-morning, there came the familiar knock at the door. I opened it and she was in my arms – as before, but not as before. In a blue woollen dress, she was beautiful and vulnerable, but no longer my Cossack, and standing back to look at me, she saw not her sunburnt subaltern but a pale student in a tweed jacket. As if to reassure herself that I was the same person, she touched the scar – *her* scar – under my chin with a tentative finger-tip, and with something of the same motivation, I cupped my right hand round her left breast.

'No, please, not that,' she said.

Only then did I realize that, for all our paradisal past, we had no future. Hazel had faced that fact in September, but kept her darkness to herself, hoping (I believe) that new faces and new surroundings would ease my transition to the necessary new life. And so they had, and would again. In the meantime, however, her visit was for both of us a day-trip to hell.

Merciful amnesia has edited out most of the detail from the memory-footage of those hours. We drove to Watlington for lunch with friends from Nigeria. The talk there was of people and beaches and horses we had known together – every name a nail in the coffin of a shared life. Returning to Oxford in the dark, we said goodbye (*adieu* masquerading as *au revoir*) in a misty carpark. I had never felt so lonely, so guilty, or so sad.

Those feelings recurred some time later when, translating the *Aeneid*, Book VI, I followed Aeneas to the Underworld and came, with a shock of recognition, to a region

Where those consumed by the wasting torments of merciless love
Haunt the sequestered alleys and myrtle groves that give them
Cover; death itself cannot cure them of love's disease.

. . .

Amongst them, with her death-wound still bleeding, through the
    deep wood
Was straying Phoenician Dido. Now when the Trojan leader
Found himself near her and knew that the form he glimpsed
    through the shadows
Was hers – as early in the month one sees, or imagines he sees,
Through a wrack of cloud the new moon rising and
    glimmering –
He shed some tears, and addressed her in tender, loving tones: –
Poor, unhappy Dido, so the message was true that came to me,
Saying you'd put an end to your life with the sword and were
    dead?
Oh god! Was it death I brought you, then? I swear by the stars,
By the powers above, by whatever is sacred in the Underworld,
It was not of my own will, Dido, I left your land.
Heaven's commands, which now force me to traverse the shades,
This sour and derelict region, this pit of darkness, drove me
Imperiously from your side. I did not, could not imagine

My going would ever bring such terrible agony on you.
Don't move away! Oh, let me see you a little longer!
To fly from me, when this is the last word fate allows us!

Painful though I found this passage, I can see now that indirectly it brought comfort, showing me how to put my misery to practical use. I would write Hazel a long poem framing and developing some of the short ones I had written her. It would be a 'secret' poem, its secret one that only she and I would understand; a poem at once celebration and elegy. I knew how it would begin, but didn't ask myself how it would end. I knew its stanza-form: the one Spenser had invented for his consciously archaic romance, *The Faerie Queene*, and Keats adopted for his, 'The Eve of St Agnes'. I thought I would call it 'The Tides of Love', but no sooner had I started than I discovered that the 1956 subject for the university's Newdigate Poem prize was 'The Deserted Altar'. Since my head was full of Virgilian altars and Desertion was an aspect of my story, I decided to enter.

My story began with 'her' leaving her friends on the beach, finding 'him' asleep on a little hill, and beside him a poem. As she reads it, he wakens.

> Alone she came the next time to those sands,
>   And in his arms, was from her tossed canoe
> Rough-cradled to the shore. Long, with linked hands
>   They wandered where the spray's brief rainbow blew,
>   And when the wave hissed home, stepped light-foot through.
> The world and the world's rages fell behind.
>   Only each other and the hour they knew;
> And when the day to a starred dusk declined,
> She went with words remembered lapping in her mind
>
>   . . .
>
> So noon by noon their love flamed into flower,
>   A love no nearer to the world than they
> Who to the sweet lees drained the brimming hour.

She asked him at the ebb of such a day,
    When idling in the sea's white lips they lay;
'Weave such a song for me, as I may wear
    Alone in my long night when worlds away.'
  At the stars' gathering, his voices there
Went out upon a stripling wind that teased her hair.

(He writes her the sonnet 'Riding the waves white-saddled
under the moon'.)*

Silent, she gave him kisses with closed eyes,
    Unnumbered as the strewn sands where they lay:
But sensing on his heart the lips' disguise;
    'Tell me,' she whispered . . . faint and far away
    The surf stormed on the reefs . . . He said: 'Today
In worlds beyond our wall, went out for me
    The summons I have feared and must obey.
  Now runs the night upon us. Though it be
More desolate in the darkness than the whelming sea,

Between our sorrows and the bitter moon
    Vines of forgetfulness will surely grow,
And grapes of comfort come to season soon.
    Barbed winds around us into sleep shall blow,
    Who saw not for the sun what now we know:
There is no star so fixed it cannot fall.
    When in these footprints, lulled with time you go,
  Only the hours of our delight recall;
In these remember me, and you remember all.'

She did not weep, but quieter than before
    And seaward-looking, whispered: 'So it ends.
How, when the steepled wave uplifts no more
    Its foam-veined shoulder to our coupled hands,
    And we two print no longer these pale sands –

* See pp. 142–3.

How will you hold me in your vision's core?
   My image to your heart bind in with bands
Of this night's forging.' And the moonrise saw
Their round of love completed by the sounding shore.

Beneath their hill, tempestuous, the tide
   Rode down each curving of the wind-ribbed sand;
For whom, in mastery unsatisfied,
   They had no eyes, nor might then understand
   The surge and slack of love. A star's fine strand
Swept Heaven's cheek with fire. She murmured: 'See!
   An angel tumbles to the breathless land,
Robbed of his wings of immortality –'
The tide, its fury tamed, slid back upon the sea.

He left her in sleep dappled with pale dreams
   When yet the dawn was foreign to the skies;
And looks on her in torment, who it seems
   Broken upon his art's cold altar lies.

. . .

And still she lingered in the arms of sleep,
   Smiled, while her roof of Heaven tumbled round;
And in the sharp rinse of the dawn-lit deep
   He sought to cleanse his sickness. But the sound
   Of her quiet breathing would not so be drowned.
Out to the beaches' limit though he fled
   There too it followed. He returning, found
Only her impress on their hill-high bed,
And his wind-wandering verses at whose end he read:

'If you have ever loved me, let your song
   Return once more: nor think of me so ill
That I who held your heart-abundance long
   Should live for less.' He flung him from the hill
   Calling her name, but far and faster still
Her footprint and his shadow flew before.
   Only salt-fleeces meet him; where they fill,
Drain, fret and dull the last dints on the shore
Of one who ran and laughed and loved, and would no more.

He saw her in his vision, under sea
   Dandled where fish through caverned coral swim,
And green weed garlands on her; drifting free
    Out of his arms upon the current's whim
    As the slack ocean, without thought of him.
Reaching his fingers where her fanned hair curled
   She slipped his grasp, as Dido down the dim
Fantastic mazes of an unseen world,
Where is no tide, nor changing nor the loud surf hurled.

Insensate there and all his voices dumb,
   But one that whispered, whispered 'So it ends',
He long awaited what he knew must come.
    Not as of old with singing and her friends
    She came to him; but on a wave that blends
Her tresses with its own. Cold was he too
   Who laid her in the boat where sand descends,
And caught the combing wash. Their frail canoe
Hurtled against the loom of surf and lifted through.

The fire-wash of his paddle danced beyond
   One instant under that devouring night,
Which bound him to her with so tight a bond
    As never dawn shall loosen. There unite
    Her love, his voices and their linked delight,
Who now together, wave in wave belong
   Till deeps yield up their dead. From sense and sight
Their altar fell: the beaten grass grew long,
Forgetful of her warmth, nor mindful of his song.

★

When I ask myself why they both had to die, the obvious answer
is: she, because Dido did; he, because I didn't want to appear a
cold-hearted Aeneas. At a deeper level, however, I think I was
telling myself that Hazel and I had to be dead to each other. I
didn't show her the poem, presumably because I couldn't explain
– or didn't want to explain – why I had killed her.

I did send a draft to Tosswill. His response, combining encouragement with constructive criticism, shows why he was such an inspiring teacher:

1. The technique, both in the Spenserian stanzas and the lyrics, seems to me remarkably secure.
2. The smoothness (one result of the above) is perhaps a little dangerous.
3. There is seldom a wrong word, apart from an occasional archaism like 'flings him': on the other hand, there are few 'surprising, but intellectually right' words.
4. One can hardly generalise about these things, but I would say that the subject is drawn too much from literary recollections: the feeling of passion – horrid word! – is rarely there.
5. I would suggest much Yeats, and perhaps practice with the short story – both in aid of economy and exactness.

We exchanged a few letters about specific revisions, after which I typed up a fair copy. I gave this an epigraph (from Rupert Brooke's sonnet, 'Waikiki'):

> . . . a tale I have heard or known . . .
> Of two that loved – or did not love – and one
> Whose perplexed heart did foolishly,
> A long while since and by some other sea.

Entries for the Newdigate Prize had to be submitted under a pseudonym. I chose 'Phlebas the Phoenician'* (perhaps to counter any impression that I thought modern poetry ended with Rupert Brooke) and handed in 'his' poem at the University Offices.

*

* Phlebas the Phoenician, a fortnight dead
  Forgot the cry of gulls, and the deep sea swell
  And the profit and loss.
     T.S. Eliot, *The Waste Land*, 1922, lines 312–14.

My first sightings and soundings of Oxford's other undergraduate poets were disappointing. I liked their poems in the university magazines less than what I knew of the work of their predecessors, particularly Keith Douglas and Sidney Keyes, and I didn't warm to those I met. They talked too loudly of poems accepted by prestigious London magazines and of parties at Faber and Faber. Most of this was wishful fiction, but I didn't know that, and feeling outclassed I kept my distance. I now regret this: in particular, my failure to meet the one poet who *did* seem 'the real thing'. Unlike the others, Richard Selig was truly glamorous. Strikingly handsome, he had worked as a merchant seaman before coming to Oxford, as an American Rhodes Scholar, to read English at Magdalen. His poems *did* appear in prestigious London magazines and very impressive I thought them. I was no less impressed by his fiancée, the beautiful Irish harpist Mary O'Hara, who was then taking harmony lessons from the Magdalen Organ Scholar, Dudley Moore.

Our Puck, our Cherubino, Dudley was the star attraction of every worthwhile party in Magdalen; gravitating towards the piano, there to invent or refine the comic routines soon to become famous in *Beyond the Fringe*. He played the organ at evensong in chapel and was responsible for a marked increase in the size of its congregation. At the end of a service, the college President, Tom Boase, would pause in the antechapel to hear the start of the organist's voluntary. After a few minutes, it being time to dress for dinner, he would leave. As soon as Dudley saw him go (in the organist's mirror), the voluntary would 'suffer a sea-change Into something rich and strange'. Handel, Purcell, Mozart would modulate into syncopated anticipations of Scott Joplin and set an enlarged congregation swaying like a wheatfield in the wind.

I had other musical friends: David Lloyd-Jones, directing choirs all over Oxford, and Richard Sorabji, rapidly mastering the Spanish guitar my father had given him for his twenty-first birthday. Richard had a fine tenor voice and a repertoire of cabaret songs that soon included some I wrote for him. The first, 'A Magdalen Gargoyle', was sung to the tune of the Eton Boating Song:

He was only a Magdalen gargoyle
And he hadn't a gargirl friend,
Yet he loved the President's daughter
From his windy cornice end.
But his features provoked derision
And the tourists would point and jeer:
While the pigeons obscured his vision
Whenever his love came near.

At the Magdalen commemoration
Ran tears on his cheeks of stone,
As he longed for the incarnation
When *he* would be flesh and bone:
And the couples went whirling below him –
His idol was there with a don –
And he only could pour out a poem,
Though he'd nothing to pour it on.

His Gog mother had compunction
As she happened to fly across,
And she said: 'You shall go to the function
In your gloves and your tails of moss.
But gloves you must always have on you,
For your hands will be cold as snow.'
And he swore that he wouldn't be Non-U
As he climbed to the ball below.

They danced to the edge of the morning
For the don had gone home in pique,
And just as the day was dawning
She suddenly kissed his cheek.
The experience petrified her;
So what could the gargoyle do
But establish himself beside her
On a pediment made for two.

This was followed by an Oxfordized 'Frankie and Johnny':

> Frankie and Johnny were freshmen
> Though not so fresh as most:
> They had no thought for the flesh then
> And their virtue was their boast.
> *When it began, they meant no wrong.*

It would be some years before I would notice that in both these *jeux d'esprit*, as in 'The Deserted Altar', a man is responsible for the death of a woman. The double shadow of myself and Hazel extended further than I knew.

The only shadow I was aware of, however, was that of approaching exams when, one spring morning, I came face to face in the High Street with a girl I had met at dances before going to Nigeria: Jill – that was it – Jill Waldock. The first thing I noticed about her now was her hat. It was blue, woollen, and decidedly comical – but when she smiled I forgot about the hat. She had the wide smile and something of the elfin grace of Audrey Hepburn, then my ideal of feminine beauty.

If she had left home five minutes later; if I had paused to admire the brocade waistcoats in the bow window of Hall Bros. The Tailors; if. But we arrived on cue to exchange our humdrum questions and answers:

'What are you doing now?'

'Working for *The Economist*'s book review section.'

'In London?'

'Yes, but I come home most weekends.'

I should have liked to continue our conversation over a cup of coffee, but with the dark doors of the Examination Schools about to open for me like the jaws of hell in a medieval fresco, I'm not sure I would have offered Audrey Hepburn herself a cup of coffee that morning. Assuming, however, that after a week's ordeal one would be regurgitated alive, I asked her to come to a celebratory party with me and she agreed.

When the paper-warriors emerged from Grendel's Mere and

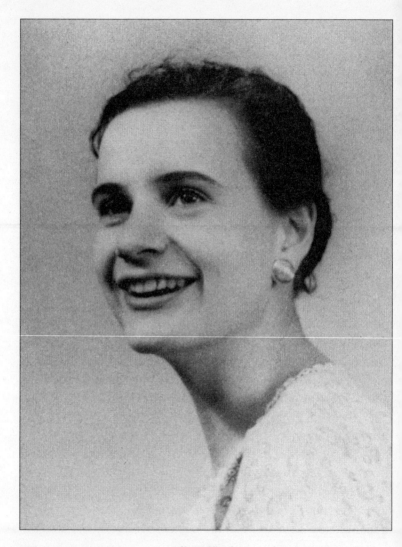

Jill Waldock

Virgil's Underworld, it was to a season of celebration. First, there was the simple fact of our survival to celebrate; then, the appearance of our names on the list of those who had 'satisfied the examiners'. Many of my ex-servicemen friends were turning 21 and hardly a weekend passed without a party or two. Meanwhile, for those who like myself had missed an English Spring, there was the spectacle of the great plane tree at the corner of Magdalen deer park coming into leaf for the hundred and fifty-fifth time, and the fritillaries hanging out their purple and white lanterns in the Great Meadow.

A minor tributary of the Cherwell loiters under the walls and bridges of Magdalen, and like Yeats (whom, on Tosswill's recommendation, I was now reading) I would

> count those feathered balls of soot
> The moorhen guides upon the stream,

knowing from my schooldays up-river how fox and pike can take their toll. In late April, the moorhens were joined by a freshly varnished flotilla of Magdalen punts, and we began to plan our part in the great public celebration of the college year. By tradition, before dawn on 1 May, its choristers climb to the top of Magdalen tower and, when the sun shows its face over Shotover Hill, they greet it with a hymn to Mithras. Then, as the last notes of this die away, the bells immediately below them break out in a wild peal and, far below on Magdalen Bridge, an accordion calls the Morris dancers into line.

Richard Sorabji and I planned a breakfast party. The guest list posed no problem. Richard, with a Rajah's fantasies of playing the Great Game in the foothills of the Himalayas, would take a beautiful Russian (was she called Olga Palovsky?), and I would invite Jill. She and I by now were comfortable in each other's undemanding company: at 17, she was in no hurry for her first love affair, any more than I was for my second.

I spent most of the last night of April in a well-provisioned Magdalen punt, with a frying pan to keep me company and a blanket to keep me warm. Neither was ideal, but shortly after four I moved the punt to the eastern side of the bridge and things began to look up. Jill and Olga arrived to share the blanket and take over from the frying pan. Then Richard came aboard with his guitar and, at his soft serenade, the tower which had been a shadow on the night sky became a shape rising out of the river mist that all but obscured the bridge. I thought of Matthew Arnold:

> And the first grey of morning fill'd the east,
> And the fog rose out of the Oxus stream.
> But all the Tartar camp along the stream
> Was hush'd, and still the men were plunged in sleep;
> Sohrab alone, he slept not . . .

As 6 o'clock approached, he stopped singing and the huddled masses in the punts around us fell silent, all waiting for the bat-like voices from the upper air. We *thought* we heard them. We certainly heard the bells. Then the puntsmen stood to their poles and, when the log-jam cleared, we moved up-river.

>   Soon a hum arose,
> As of a great assembly loosed, and fires
> Began to twinkle through the fog, for now
> Both armies moved to camp, and took their meal . . .

Richard and I had chosen a mooring and campsite in advance and, while I took charge of the fire and the women put the frying pan to work, he regaled other ships' companions beside his own with a medley of ballads, sea shanties, and the Volga Boatmen's Song.

The promise of that luminous dawn was abundantly fulfilled in the term that followed: mornings in tutorial, listening to Emrys Jones anatomize texts with a subtlety that brought them alive as never before; afternoons in a library, trying to anticipate his examination of the texts for the next week; evenings in a punt arguing about poetry. This was Keith Douglas's 'Oxford':

> At home, as in no other city, here
> summer holds her breath in a dark street

the trees nocturnally scented, lovers like moths
go by silently on the footpaths
and spirits of the young wait
cannot be expelled, multiply each year.

In the meadows, walks, over the walls
the sunlight, far-travelled, tired and content,
warms the recollections of old men, touching
the hand of the scholar on his book, marching
through the quadrangles and arches, at last spent
it leans through the stained windows and falls.

★

The end of term brought the fulfilment of another promise, one
made at Rugby two years before: that, if we survived National
Service and our 'first public examination' at Oxford, David
Cocks and I would treat ourselves to a holiday in Spain. Why
Spain? I fancy we thought Spain more colourful than France and
cheaper than Italy. Both considerations were important. We had
each saved some money during National Service (David as a
'Gunner' in Germany), but not enough for a holiday. What made
it possible was my mother's generous loan of her ancient Morris
Oxford. 'It'll do me good to *walk* about town,' she said, which
made her family smile, as she usually *trotted* about like a little
pony.

David and I set off on 4 July and by midnight, my diary tells
me, were 235 miles nearer Spain and 780 francs poorer (the cost
of a celebratory supper in Abbeville). For the next four weeks,
that wine-stained witness lists our more modest expenses and, by
contrast, the colours on which we feasted hungry eyes. 'Lunched
on the roadside among cornflowers and poppies – peasants in
faded blue overalls'; 'houses roofed with scalloped tiles of orange,
red, and an increasingly pale tint of pink as we went southward'.
Trailing a plume of white dust, we climbed through many hairpin
bends into Andorra, then descended through many hairpin bends

into Spain. In Barcelona, still hungry for colour, we went to a bullfight:

> trumpets – parade of bull-fighters up to the red-and-yellow-flagged president's box. Door swings back and a black bull hurtles into the ring – glances left, pauses, charges right at pink cape men who retire behind the barricades. Mounted picadors, horses one-eye-blind-folded, crudely quilted, lance bull's shoulder – flutter of red ribbon – clang of thrusting horn on iron stirrup boxes – trumpets – exit picadors. Six bright *banderillas* stuck in on the run – blood welling on dark flank. A matador slithers down – bull whirls round on him, sand spurting from its hooves – vicious head butting low ploughs the sand on either side – bull diverted by trail, swirl, and lure of pink capes. Matador's hand bandaged, he stalks arrogantly away from encircling barricade – kicks his black hat aside, throws down the white bandage. Drag and pawing of hooves – the bull rushes at the scarlet cloak, *banderillas* flailing both flanks. Matador, hand on hip, leaning over the lurch of the charging bull – wide gold epaulettes glitter in the failing sun – kneels to the bull – the crowd roaring '*Olé!*' at every pass – statuesque, spinning like a ballet dancer, sword drawn from cape – lunge with straight arm, head back. Bull squats suddenly pathetic to its haunches, coughs, rolls over – ears and tail cut off – matador towels his head, accepts them, prances round the ring. Flowers, fans, wineskins. Carcass dragged out by three jingling decorated horses – sand raked smooth. Five more bulls – some good passes, some bad – all dead, the last roaring.

That night we pitched our tent on a seemingly deserted beach and, with poetic justice, were tormented by *banderilla*-bearing mosquitoes.

★

In cafés, in the car, in our tent, we talked of many things, but of nothing more than poetry. Although David was now reading Law, he had won an exhibition to New College as an English specialist and was a better critic than I. He was also a challeng-

ing talker with a fine sardonic wit, who sent me burrowing for
evidence to support my arguments: as, for example, that Dylan
Thomas was an important poet. I had brought his *Collected Poems*
and John Malcolm Brinnin's *Dylan Thomas in America*, and was
intoxicated with the music of the poems.

'Isn't it just bardic blarney?' asked David. 'What's behind it?'

Looking more carefully at the poems, I began to see the
formal beauty and intricacy of their construction: how the
'vowel rhymes' of 'Fern Hill' (b*o*ughs/t*o*wns, gr*ee*n/l*ea*ves)
contribute unobtrusively to its music, and how the fluent movement of its lines masks a rigid grid of syllables:

Now as I was young and easy under the apple boughs   *(14)*
About the lilting house and happy as the grass was green,   *(14)*
   The night above the dingle starry,   *(9)*
     Time let me hail and climb   *(6)*
   Golden in the heydays of his eyes,   *(9)*
And honoured among wagons I was prince of the apple towns *(15)*
And once below a time I lordly had the trees and leaves   *(14)*
   Trail with daisies and barley   *(7)*
   Down the rivers of the windfall light.   *(9)*

'Why does there have to be a rigid grid of syllables?' asked
David.

I said I supposed it was because the poem was about an Edenic
childhood, much of its movement was circular, and Eden was a
place of perfect proportions.

Together we discovered Lorca. I had brought the recently
published *Penguin Book of Spanish Verse*, and one of us must have
brought – or found in a Spanish bookshop – his *Lament for the
Death of a Bullfighter and Other Poems*, splendidly translated by
A.L. Lloyd (my diary refers to Lloyd's titles). Our experience of
the bullfight gave us a context for Lorca's 'Lament':

    Already the bull is bellowing within his head
    at five in the afternoon.

The room is iridescent with agony
at five in the afternoon.
Now from afar comes gangrene
at five in the afternoon,
a lily-trumpet through greenish groins
at five in the afternoon.
His wounds blazed like suns
at five in the afternoon,
and the rabble shattered the windows
at five in the afternoon.
At five in the afternoon.
Ay, that terrible five o'clock in the afternoon!
It was five by all the clocks!
It was five in the shadow of the afternoon!

We rolled the sumptuous Spanish round our mouths like a vintage wine, and scarcely a day would pass without our chanting in chorus:

A las cinco de la tarde.
¡Ay, qué terribles cinco de la tarde!
¡Eran las cinco en todos los relojes!
¡Eran las cinco en sombra de la tarde!

My closer reading of Thomas and Lorca, Blake and Yeats (who were also travelling with us), was making me more critical of my own poems, and there are pages of the diary crossstitched with useless revisions of 'Camaret *en Fête*' and 'The Deserted Altar'; useless, because I had still to learn how to sew new cloth into an old garment without making the rent worse. My motives for attempting to revise the older poem may well have been extra-literary. Remembering 'bare brown ankles rising, falling', I had written to Jacqueline (of the Camaret holiday), asking whether she and her parents would take in two travellers on their way back to England. They received us royally. Jacqueline was entrancing, but now far too sophisticated to be swayed by an unsophisticated schoolboy poem so, saving us both embarrassment, it was still in my luggage when we headed for home.

★

Early in September, sensing the year about to turn, I took out my rugger boots and dubbined them lovingly. Rubbing the grease into pliant leather with my thumb, I imagined strikes 'against the head' (the ball put into the scrum by the opposing scrum-half), match-saving tackles, and match-winning tries. A month's hard training with the Oxford Rugby Football Club brought me down to earth, but at the end of it I was chosen to play for the city club against a University team picked, by tradition, by that year's captain of the OURFC. The 1956 captain was Olwyn Brace, a Welsh International scrum-half, and his team included five old Blues (two of them also Internationals).

It was a good game – fast, hard, and clean – and at half time the University was leading 6–3. In the second half, the local team counter-attacked strongly, and, at the final whistle, were 9–6 ahead. I was encouraged to read in the *Manchester Guardian* next morning that 'Oxford owed their success in the main to Stallworthy's skilful hooking, which made it possible for Coles, a resourceful scrum-half, to make full use of the speed and thrust of his backs.'

The following week, I was in the University's Final Trial, but when the *Oxford Mail* reported that 'Neither of the four hookers seen was of the required class', I could fault the grammar but not the judgement. That Saturday, my services were required by neither the OURFC nor the second team, the OU Greyhounds.

The double rejection concentrated my mind wonderfully and when, to my amazement and delight, I was asked to play for the Greyhounds in their annual match against the University on 30 October, my father said he would take the afternoon off, and I knew what I had to do.

That day the University fielded seven old Blues – one of

them, John Rigby, in the front row – but in such encounters the underdogs have a psychological advantage, and never more so than when led by such a captain as J.E. Close: 1956 was 'Chopper' Close's last chance to win a Blue, which he was determined to do, taking as many other underhounds with him as possible. In our Iffley Road changing-room, his pre-match pep-talk was Churchillian. We would fight them in the tight, in the loose, in the lineout, under their posts and ours. Not only would we never surrender, we would eat them alive, and do the same to Cambridge at Twickenham in five weeks' time. His conviction, his rhetoric, had a Churchillian effect. When the hands of the changing-room clock came round to 2.30 and the referee knocked on our door to ask if we were ready, Chopper led us out like a bull into the bull-ring.

I was lucky to have to my immediate left and right in the shield-wall the red-hot Chopper and Dennis McLean, a New Zealand Rhodes Scholar, whose metal had been tempered in the furnace of New Zealand provincial rugby. These two led a charge that threw the University off balance, but even so they scored first, Malcolm Phillips (who would later play for England) racing over our line for an unconverted try. A minute or two later, our full-back levelled the score with a penalty goal – both were then worth three points – and, almost at once, the University's right wing, John Young ·(who would also play for England), pulled a thigh muscle and had to leave the field.

We were now winning the ball in the tight and in the loose, and our backs began to scythe down – and scythe through – their opposition. A Greyhound centre scored a try and then a wing, finding his way forward blocked, passed inside to the tireless Chopper, who hurled himself over the line for a captain's try. The crowd rose to their feet and clapped till their hands must have ached. I could see my father, his bedside manner quite forgotten, shouting with the rest. At half-time, we were leading 11–3. After the interval, a tide of dark blue jerseys threatened to overrun the field, but a grey breakwater held and repelled it and

Oxford University 11, Oxford University Greyhounds 17. Far left,
two hookers in fraternal embrace

when, in fading light, the last whistle went, the Greyhounds had
won by 17 points to 11.

'By God,' said Chopper as he led us off the field, 'they'll
have to make some changes.'

★

Tom Boase used to say that, since newspaper reports of anything
of which he had first-hand knowledge were invariably inaccurate, he could only assume that *all* newspaper reports were inaccurate. Admiring his parade of worldly cynicism, I would
sometimes steal his lines, but not on the morning after the match
when the *Manchester Guardian* said of our victory: 'The forwards
responded untiringly to the zestful leadership of Close. . . .
Stallworthy's quick striking, supported by sound scrummaging,
also enabled the Greyhound forwards to heel quicker and more
smoothly if not so often as their opponents.' The qualification
was fair: my opposite number 9, Jack Hoare, was a more expe-
rienced, more reliable hooker than I was (and would play in an
England Trial).

The Times said: 'it cannot be hidden that if [the Greyhounds] had changed their grey jerseys for dark blue they would have looked more like a good university side in the making'. The following week, four of our team – three outsides and a back-row forward – did change their grey jerseys for dark blue. We never recovered from their loss and, on 6 December, were soundly beaten, 28–3, by the Cambridge LX Club (that University's second XV). Five days later, their first XV defeated ours, 14–9, at Twickenham.

These disappointments were soon forgotten in an uproarious pre-Christmas OURFC tour to the South of France on which I deputized for Jack Hoare, who was working for his exams. In between gargantuan meals, we played three matches: against Sélection de Languedoc (a good win), Mazamet (a painful defeat), and Union Sportif de Montaubonoise (a pleasant win).

The Old English poet was not the only member of the shield-wall with an ear for poetry, and a friend (who would later captain Wales) confirms that this situation had not changed in a thousand years. Robin Davies writes:

> At Narbonne, I had my first encounter with 'Bagpipe Music',* which John Rigby recited in bed from a book of poems borrowed from Brian Weston (no forward, with your honourable exception, would have been so sensibly equipped in those days).

Blessed with a memory better than mine, he continues:

> After the Blanchette de Limoux, I recall some forty or fifty of us packed into a small convivial room with our cigars and great excitement to see 'Le striptease'. The good lady took one look round the door at this highly emotional party and fled!

My memory recovers with the match against Mazamet. After ten minutes, we were leading by a dropped goal and two scorch-

* By Louis MacNeice.

ing tries to nil: both tries scored by Malcolm Phillips. Making a third break, however, he was felled by a murderous straight-arm tackle, the law of levers dropping him flat on his back with a badly cut mouth. The local referee overlooked the incident; not so our captain, Peter Robbins, the best wing-forward in England. He waited until Malcolm's assailant next received the ball and saw to it that he simultaneously received fourteen stone of bone and muscle travelling at cannon-ball velocity. It was a fair tackle, but it ignited the game. The referee had a simple solution: every time he saw a flailing fist or boot – no matter what colour the sleeve or sock behind it – he awarded a penalty to Mazamet. Oxford lost 11–16.

By the time we came to Montaubon, the stokers in the engine-room of the scrum were accustomed to the heat and acclimatized to its miasma of stale garlic, Gauloises, and sweat. The game was better-tempered, we played better, and won (I think) 9–3.

★

A sheet of blue notepaper among my fixture-cards shows that, on tour, my mind was not fixed solely on the next scrum or the next meal. It is headed:

LE *Grand Balcon*

ALLO 1347

MAZAMET
(TARN)   FRANCE
CENTRE DE TOURISME
CAPITALE MONDIALE
DU DÉLAINAGE

UNE AMBIANCE JEUNE ET SYMPATHIQUE DANS UN CADRE AGRÉABLE

Son Restaurant réputé
Ses Chambres grand Confort
Son Bar

Under this, an undergraduate hand has drafted several stanzas from the middle of a long poem.

Having had no success with 'The Deserted Altar', and

mindful of Keats's dictum that 'a long poem is a test of Invention, which I take to be the polar star of poetry', I was at work on another entry for the Newdigate Prize. The 1957 subject was 'Leviathan' and I was launched into an allegorical narrative based on the biblical story of Jonah and the whale. Subtitled 'The journey in search of a purpose', this reflected a barely acknowledged concern about my own lack of purpose. As long as I could remember I had looked forward to university, but I hadn't looked beyond it. What was I going to DO – apart from writing poems, which I knew wouldn't DO as a career? I pushed the thought away and, recalling Norfolk mornings 'before the mast', pushed out another boat:

> With the ripple and rush
> Of halyard in block, they hauled up the morning, hand
> Swung over hand. On forearm and shoulder the flush
> Of the sun spread, as it ramped through the rigging manned
> With birds: and the chant of the crew flamed through the hush
>
> Of the wakening bay.
> The decks are running thunder and a white cloud swells
> From the mast, high-bosomed. In the sprung bud of day,
> Singing, they left the quay on a tide of bells,
> Past the boats lying seaward down the white-gulled way.

I knew (but wasn't troubled by the knowledge) that both the stanza-form and the narrator's voice were Dylan Thomas's. Tosswill, to whom I sent a draft of 200 lines of 'ancient' narrative – into which I planned to splice a 'modern' allegory – recommended a significant change of course:

This is a much better poem than 'The Deserted Altar'; how good it's hard to say, because the *really* important parts are those you've not yet written. These should presumably be rather more formal in style than the narrative passages. And incidentally should be *longer* than the 90 lines you propose – otherwise the proportions will (I feel) be all wrong: this should *not* be pre-eminently narrative. So either you should compress what you've already written, or expand your 90.

I'd suggest the former, since there is a decline in quality after the first 2 pages – which are excellent. Later you seem to tire: much is loose and insufficiently emphatic. So either it must be tightened or cut.

Some phrases (other than the ones I marked) are too consciously Dylan: they don't *really* say what you feel. But in correcting them, preserve the clarity of syntax at all costs; since in many ways that's the best thing about the poem . . .

I knew he was right, but couldn't bring myself to prune the narrative as radically as he recommended. When, in February, I sent him a draft of the complete poem, he wrote:

I still feel that narrative out-weighs what you call 'intestine', and that you should add to the latter . . .

My only general criticism is that [the poem] is over-imaged or, to be more precise, over-metaphored à la Dylan. There aren't enough visible bones. Before making your final decisions, it might help if you looked at 'The Wreck of the Deutschland' and 'Moby Dick' – though I expect you know them better than I do [*of course I didn't*].

A postscript to his letter suggests one reason why I failed to follow advice which I knew to be sound: 'I watch your progress to a Rugger Blue with delight.' The spring term was under way and I was playing with the dark blue team once or twice a week.

There was another distraction. The Junior Common Room had to elect a President for the following year, the college's Quincentenary. Kenneth Baker, a polished pillar of the Oxford University Conservative Association, declared his candidacy. A hero of the Left came forward to challenge him. Both were strongly supported, but there were others in the college who were unhappy at the prospect of a take-over by either political party. At the height of the Suez crisis the previous year, the JCR had debated – and roundly rejected – a motion that 'this house is willing to discuss matters of politics and religion and to express an opinion on them as a corporate body'.

It was suggested that I should enter the lists as an independent candidate, and having (in those days) a troublesome propensity to say yes rather than no, I agreed. When the votes were cast and counted, it emerged that the Blue Knight and the Red Knight had unhorsed each other, leaving a be-mused Green Knight master of the field. I had also said yes to the offer of an English-Speaking Union Fellowship that would take me to a number of American universities in the Easter vacation. As term ended, I dubbined my rugger boots, polished my poem, and on 19 March delivered a fair copy (beautifully typed by Jill) to the University Registrar's counter before racing to London airport.

My pulse raced for the next five weeks, as – learning the language of baseball – I made what I came to think of as an exhilarating 'home run': from Princeton to Yale, Georgetown, William and Mary, Virginia, Harvard, and back to Princeton. On the way round, I saw *Tosca* at the Met, Solti conducting at Carnegie Hall, ice-hockey at Madison Square Stadium. I went to the Library of Congress, the Chesterfield Cigarette Factory, Jefferson's Montecello, Colonial Williamsburg, and the Deep Run Races. I was never in bed before midnight. I fell in love with America and Americans, and returned with no poems, but many traveller's tales. These, however, paled beside those my parents brought back at the same time from South Africa.

There was my mother's account of an incident, versions of which I would hear from many sources over many years. My father had agreed to lecture and demonstrate operations at a number of major centres on the explicit, written, understanding that he would only appear before multi-racial audiences. In one hospital, with a smart new demonstration theatre and spectators' gallery, he was asked to perform an operation never before performed in South Africa. He found the proposed (white) patient anxious to undergo a procedure which, all being well, would transform her life, and agreed to operate the following day.

That evening, he had dinner with an Indian doctor and, as he was leaving, said: 'I'll see you tomorrow.'

'No, I'm afraid you won't,' his friend replied.

'Aren't you coming to the Wertheim?'*

'No.'

'Why not?'

'I'm not allowed.'

'Why not?'

'Only Whites are admitted.'

My father immediately telephoned the Head of the Department to say there had been some mistake. The voice on the other end of the phone was embarrassed and apologetic. No, there was no mistake: the bye-laws expressly forbade non-White doctors from attending operations on White patients.

'Then I shan't operate,' said my father.

'But the patient's been prepared for surgery that she believes will change her life. You can't disappoint her.'

My father saw that he was trapped and agreed to operate – but under protest.

Next day, the operation went to plan until, in its later stages, a theatre sister passed the surgeon a needle and thread. He looked at it a long moment. Then, pulling down his mask with his right hand, he raised needle and thread in his left and, addressing the crowded gallery, asked: 'Am I allowed to use black thread on a White woman?' There was a great silence, after which my father replaced his mask and sewed up the wound.

★

My second summer term at Oxford was the best. Our first public exams were far behind us, our second far ahead. Richard had new songs – as well as his old ones – with which to welcome Mithras on May Morning, and a new partner at his side: Kate

* I *think* the operation was a Wertheim, but could be wrong.

Taster, an undergraduate reading English at Lady Margaret Hall. Together we would celebrate many things – birthdays, nights of full moon, my 'Leviathan' coming second in the Newdigate.

When a foursome seemed too many, Jill and I would borrow my mother's car and drive out to a favourite stretch of the River Windrush. There was a gravel-bottomed pool where we could swim, secluded banks on which to picnic and learn more (but not everything) about each other.

In October, as President of the JCR, I moved into a suite of great splendour in the Magdalen Cloisters. It had been adapted for Edward Prince of Wales during his years at Oxford, and boasted a bathroom (a rare, if not unique, feature in Oxford undergraduate accommodation at the time). A large sitting-room overlooked the lawns in front of the eighteenth-century New Buildings, and a bedroom window framed the tower. The true master of these palatial premises was not the ephemeral president but the permanent scout. He was called Ireland and aspired to the gravitas and tact of a Royal Servant.

When for a week he had not made my bed, I asked him (with as much tact as an Anglo-antipodean commoner could muster) why. Very gravely he inclined his long lugubrious head towards the bedroom door and silently withdrew. On it was hanging a short coat Jill had forgotten the previous weekend.

At the other end of the college – and the moral scale – was the scout who presided over rooms that took their name from their most famous occupant, Oscar Wilde. Douglas (let's call him) had perfected a routine for visiting tourists.

'And this is Mr Woilde's parlour,' he would say. 'Standin' where you are, 'e would poke 'is small coals in that foirplace. Money couldn't buy that poker!' When they re-entered the shadowy passage, sometimes someone would sidle up to him and whisper:

'I'll give you twenty dollars for that poker.'

'Oh, I couldn't sell Mr Woilde's poker . . . not for twenty dollars.' For how many dollars he could, would, and did, depended on his estimate of the fish he was playing. Once he had landed his catch, the Compleat Angler would return to his pantry and take out another Woolworth poker from his store.

★

On 22 October, turning over a page in *The Times* that I never read, two words in heavy type hit me in the eye: **Richard Selig**. Disbelieving, I read and re-read Jack Bennett's obituary:

> The many friends of the young American poet Richard Selig will be saddened by the announcement of his death [from Hodgkin's disease] in New York last week at the age of 27; none of them could have guessed from his recent poems or letters that he had known for two years that his life was likely to be brief. He was not the first Rhodes Scholar who has come to Oxford as a rebel only to leave it with filial affection; but few have transmuted such abounding vitality and such a rich love of miscellaneous experience – he had worked as a cook, a film extra, mechanic, and merchant seaman before he came to Magdalen – into poetry at once gentle and intense. Almost all of this verse was published in English magazines such as *The Listener* and *Encounter*, though some has appeared, and more is about to appear, in *Botteghe Obscure*. The last year of his life – the year of his marriage to the Irish harpist Mary O'Hara – though it closed in weeks of pain, was certainly his happiest. 'Cut is the branch that would have grown full straight.' But his last poems, reflecting in their increasing mastery of form a hard-won serenity, will be a meet memorial.

Someone else whom the gods loved. Sitting in the Common Room – perhaps the chair – where Selig had so often sat, I felt the draught of the thunderbolt.

As one Oxford poet descended to the Underworld, another emerged into the light. Dom Moraes, an Indian undergraduate at Jesus College, was 19 years old. His poems had also appeared in *Encounter* and *Botteghe Obscure*, and a first collection – mod-

estly called *A Beginning* – was published in 1957. Stephen
Spender was quoted on the dust-jacket as saying that 'His poems
have a quite peculiar tenderness and loneliness, reminiscent of
David Gascoyne.' It was easy to see why Spender found them
attractive. Moraes's 'Song' sounded like early Auden:

> The gross sun squats above
> A valley full of shadows:
> The wizard plays his flute
> And lizards in green meadows
> And archers in pursuit
> Of antelope and dove
> Grow dumb and cannot move.

Unlike most other undergradute poets, however, Moraes had
already outgrown his influences and – at 19 – had a voice and
vision of his own. Not yet knowing that envy between poets is
a compliment second only to imitation, I was shocked to find
myself envious of 'Moz', for example:

> I saw him turn to bluster, clutch his head,
> The King of Moz, his thunders launched in vain:
> The ageing Queen sank back into her bed,
> Making one final gesture of disdain.
>
> She flashed her eyes and passed beyond his yells,
> Dying from her Moz, country of talking trees,
> To strike a happy medium somewhere else.
> The King came slowly to his royal knees.
>
> A chirping twilight fell. She lay quietly.
> Priests moved their heads and lips, imploring grace.
> Her emptied eyes looked up, where in the sky
> Two stars resumed their long vacated place.
>
> Wordless, I closed my heart. Now I return,
> Amazed that stone endures and rivers move,
> And persecute my friends with smiles to learn
> Their water rates, and have they been in love.

I clench my sleep upon a thought that springs
Out of a nervous kind of fixity:
The King pacing his bedroom, touching things,
Trying vaguely to conceive eternity.

I recognized an authority and an originality far beyond anything I myself possessed at 22. How did he do it? Perhaps Indians matured earlier than Anglo-Saxons?

I would stand at my sitting-room window, remembering Richard Selig and Mary O'Hara arm in arm on the lawns below; and turn away 'Trying vaguely to conceive eternity'.

*

As with earlier autumns, I was more occupied with the physical than the metaphysical. I played for the Blues in the final trial, but then Jack Hoare returned from the library and I returned to the Greyhounds. We beat the United Services at Chatham 61–0, but lacking the inspiration of a Chopper Close, were ourselves beaten 21–3 by the University. A fortnight later, on the same Iffley Road ground, we lined up against Pontypridd. I was wearing a pair of boots that had been handmade for Ian Botting, a New Zealand All Black wing-three-quarter, and given to me when he retired. They fitted me like kid gloves – their leather was almost as supple as kid – and wearing them I felt wing-heeled.

To my surprise, I won the first scrum 'against the head', receiving a second later a sharp kick in the instep from the Welsh hooker. This happened several times more in subsequent scrums before I realized it was deliberate. My opposite number had seen that I wasn't wearing standard-issue tough toe-capped boots and, with clinical precision, was targeting my Achilles instep. I could either grin and bear it or leave the striking to him. I attempted the first, but soon could neither grin nor bear it and limped off the field with a foot like a football. My father drove me to his hospital's casualty department. There, very gently, the doctor on duty cut away my boot with surgical scissors to reveal a piece of raw meat clearly incapable of supporting a footballer again that year. I was surprised to find I regretted the damage to the boot more than the damage to the foot. My injury wouldn't cost me a Blue, unless Jack Hoare were also to be injured, and I had another project to occupy my afternoons.

★

The subject for the 1958 Newdigate Prize, 'The Earthly Paradise', had recently been announced and the shadowy outline of a poem was beginning to take shape in my head. It was prompted by a memory of lines from Book XII of *Paradise Lost*:

> Then wilt thou not be loath
> To leave this Paradise, but shalt possess
> A Paradise within thee, happier farr.

I would travel from one to the other and, as I set off, the memory of another epic came to my aid. The Bodger's note on 'The Golden Years' had led me to Cary's translation of *The Divine Comedy*,* and I borrowed Dante's stanza for the opening section of my 'Earthly Paradise':

WINTER

> In the foreshadowing of the first storm
> When cloud and mountain trembled, trembled one
> Who watched the omens of tomorrow form
>
> Dark over Eden. He saw waters run
> From blood to gold in many falls, and trees
> Take on the Autumn of the ageing sun.
>
> While mists among them deepen like slow seas
> And orchard lands halfway to Heaven drown,
> Through him a darkness travels like disease.

* See p. 95.

Until the tides had gathered the sun down,
His eyes wrestled with distance to retrace
The sunken hill. And he forgot the brown

World at his back, the wind-tormented place,
And the girl garlanded with tears, who saw
The winter only in her husband's face.

When rivers out of Eden flashed no more
High lightning lit them to the valley's end,
And rain with riddled arms ran on before.

She, wrapped that night in the outrageous wind,
Remembered lilies, though her finger-tips
Closed upon thorns: until the darkness thinned,

And Adam turning at his dream's eclipse
Saw Eden's image, like a shadow, drawn
About her sleep; and scrolled upon her lips

Such parables of peace, that each white dawn
Darkened another life. So their belief
Died with the waking and in sleep was born.

Through every incarnation of the leaf
Till dreams put on reality they went,
Seeking against the weather of their grief
A visionary garden of content.

Subsequent sections followed other Adams through other
ncarnations of the leaf and, in each, the protagonist encoun-
ered an allegorical creature. The first represented Imagination:

SPRING

Adam awakened to a dream of Spring
That kindled in a boy's quick vein;
Saw how the leopard sun upon his sill
Laid one gold paw, and missed the quarrelling
Of a dead season's rain;
For the rains had galloped over the hill.

Spring, limbed like green fire, and the umber child
Ran heart in heart by trees in flame,
Whose flowers rose over him like petalled moons.
In forests where shadow and light ran wild
And tall deer strutted tame,
The simple grass flowed greener than lagoons.

Held in a wave of wonder he was drawn
Where, like the wind, a river passed
In music among upturned trees. Alone
He knelt to the bright water, till the dawn
In benediction cast
An image quivering beside his own.

Imagination, liveried like a fawn,
That found a new earth there begun
Beneath a dew of glory, at his side
Dimpled the stream. It was a creature born
In Eden, the first sun
And windfall shadow woven in its hide.

The river ran to flame beneath its glance,
Which, like the moonrise, when it turned
Dazzled the stripling Adam with delight.
Its shadow led him on an April dance
Through pastures, where he learned
The exultation of a sky in flight.

The pastoral idyll ends when the boy's father 'set/The fawn o
revelation in the fold'. It subsequently escapes from its pen an
is lost to them both. (Forty years on, I wonder what relevance
if any, this episode had to my relationship with my own father
whose authority, kindness, and wisdom I had never knowingl
questioned.)

In the 'Summer' section following that 'Spring', an adolescen
Adam finds himself 'Breathless before a city' – 'Duns Scotus
Oxford'* twinned with Bunyan's 'Celestial City' – where he dis

---

* A sonnet by Gerard Manley Hopkins. I had evidently taken Tosswill's
advice (see p. 175).

covers an Eve with whom to re-enact the primal Fall, despite the chastening presence of 'a single swan of Reason' in the river beside them.

A principal weakness of the poem is the arbitrary equation of human faculty and allegorical creature: the swan could as fittingly have represented Imagination. I managed a better match in the 'Autumn' section, Adam there becoming a matador:

> In all arenas after, the world sees
>   His limbs confined
> To tighter cloth, Adam erect
> In splendours of the intellect.
>   And with the mind
> He swung the bulls of passion to their knees.

Eventually, he asks a rhetorical question to which history returns a painful answer:

> Could this be less than Eden: to have stilled
>   Desire, outrun
> The horned unreason to a calm
> Achieved by his destroying arm,
>   And schooled a son
> To dominate the bulls his father killed?
>
> A shadow waggon with a shadow horse
>   Stole from the town,
> On hooves that to a bridle's tune
> Trampled the white dust of the moon;
>   And looking down
> He followed between fields its shadow course.
>
> The gossip wind no gust of singing blows
>   From such as ride
> The rocking sheaves with their day done.
> They brought no harvest, but his son
>   In whose white side
> The horn-wound flowered like a fallen rose.

The rasp and jingle of the waggon blend,
    A cricket shrills;
And the carter reined his horse, for he
Heard Adam's primal elegy
    Trouble the hills,
And all the valley telling Abel's end.

After four mini-visions of 'Paradise Lost', I came in a concluding section to a happier prospect – that of the 'Paradise within' prophesied by Milton:

PARADISE

And I Jon, who am Adam and Abel,
Who saw an Eden falling every day,
Saw also the great end of Adam's fable:
Not as I thought to see it, coming down
A star tide gathered in the Milky Way
To overflow the dawn;

But rising from the raw earth unobserved,
And from the dust made flesh, that sheathes the bone.
I saw the lawns of Paradise are served
By rivers of the heart: and from that source
The Styx and the Euphrates draw alone
Each its tremendous course.

By such a river in the tidal dawn
When trees, unrooted, seemed on mist afloat,
I saw this miracle: a drinking fawn
Rise with a new coat from the stream; its old
Transfigured there, muzzle and moving throat,
Shoulder and hoof, to gold.

Then sounding down the avenues of mist,
Ghost-winged and with low thunder in its wake,
Loomed in the swan. As bird and water kissed
A rippled fan shook out and wandered far,
Linked to an image in which breast and neck
Burned silver as a star.

A bull came last, from its unrivalled herd
Searching all pastures where the river grows,
For consummation higher than the sword.
Garlands of vapour wreathed its horns in white,
And horn and hide in one fierce instant rose
Sculptured in breathing light.

A whisper, like a wind along the vein
Unfolding secrets of the fountain-head,
Stirred in me: 'Vision, Reason here regain
The lineaments and lustre of their youth;
And bulls of passion, though their horns gleam red,
Are turned as white as Truth.'

I should have ended the poem there or thereabouts, but – not for the first or last time – yielded to the temptation to make doubly explicit what should have been implicit; and visioned on for another eight stanzas. I had a complete draft to send Tosswill in early March 1958 but didn't keep his response (a sign perhaps of growing confidence).

★

While I was singing to myself, Richard was singing to his guitar and increasing audiences at cabarets and parties. One evening he was entertaining some friends in a dank, dark, and ill-attended pub when the landlord made him an offer: £1 a week (and free drink) if he would sing there three nights a week. He agreed, and soon it was one of Oxford's more popular watering-holes. The weekly payments, however, fell into arrears – Richard was too well-mannered to ask for money – until, finally, some of his friends told the landlord to pay up. He, reckoning he no longer needed a resident troubadour, told Richard and his chorus to bugger off. Far from going quietly, after Closing Time we continued to sing under his bedroom window.

Eventually, it flew open. 'I'll call the police!' he shouted.

'Yes, do!' we shouted back. 'There are half a dozen witnesses here to your breach of contract!'

The window slammed and we sang on until, in the small hours, it flew open again and three or four crisp pound notes fluttered to the ground.

That night and many others we had to climb into college. Magdalen presented no serious problem: one shinned up a lamppost beside the Long Wall battlements. This had a collar of six-inch spikes that, far from deterring climbers, gave them a hand-hold as they swung a leg over the wall. On the college side of the parapet, a white-painted ladder was permanently in place to help the benighted reach the ground.

One night, a Magdalen undergraduate was approaching the lamp-post when, to his surprise and delight, a little side-door in the wall opened to let someone out. Slipping in before the door could close, he pressed half-a-crown into the hand of a shadowy figure he took to be a night-porter.

'Young man,' said the shadow, 'next time you tip a Fellow of the College, let it be paper money!'

The voice was that of Tom Brown Stevens, an ancient historian of engaging eccentricity, who had come to the groves of Academe from an unusual direction. His ambitions as an undergraduate, he once told me, had been single-mindedly social. He cultivated the acquaintance of his titled contemporaries skilfully and, in due course, was rewarded with a crested invitation to a ducal lunch-party. Discreet enquiries of His Grace's scout elicited the information that he was to be the only commoner present. Recognizing that his role was that of entertainer, he prepared his lines like an actor in advance of the lunch that was to launch him into High Society.

The great day found him seated at his host's right hand, a fountain of wit and well-honed stories. Keeping the fountain flowing was thirsty work, but white-tied waiters saw to it that his glass was never empty. He kept the table in constant uproar. It was the début of his dreams, except for a hint of reserve on

he part of the Duke. Trying to overcome this, he redoubled his
fforts and the guests redoubled their laughter – the guests but
ot their host. And suddenly Stevens understood: the lesser
ords and Honourables were laughing not only with him but at
im, the left-handed jester draining every glass set before the
hunderously sober Duke. In that hour of humiliation, Tom
3rown Stevens understood his destiny: to wear a don's black
own in perpetual mourning for the ermine of his dreams.

My own life changed in the course – I think it was the salmon
ourse – of a humbler feast, the annual dinner of the Mermaid
Club. This was a small company of enthusiasts for Restoration
Comedy who, two or three evenings a term, read a play by
andlelight until the candles and the claret ran out.

W.H. Auden was guest of honour at our annual dinner. I had
een to all his lectures as Professor of Poetry, but lacked the
onfidence or courage to take my poems to the Cadena Café
vhere he regularly held court and commented on his courtiers'
fferings. Now, hearing him talk – more brilliantly than he lec-
ured – I regretted my cowardice. Like a jazz trumpeter riding a
ollercoaster solo, he swung into a playful typology of poets and
oetry categorized in culinary terms (or was it a culinary typol-
gy categorized in poetical terms?). Then, asked how he would
ategorize Oxford undergraduate poetry (and being too tactful
o say), he spoke of judging the Newdigate Prize. David Cocks,
vho was sitting close to him, said: 'Have the judges reached a
lecision?'

'Yes.'

'Is it X?' (He named a rumoured winner.)

'No.'

'Can you say who it is?'

'I forget the name. He's the son of an Oxford doctor.' David
ried again.

'Yes,' said Auden.

★

I had told myself I would spend the month before our final exams revising in monastic seclusion, but when my father heard that, traditionally, the Newdigate poem was printed – and offered to pay for that indulgence – I couldn't resist bowing to tradition. I had heard of a jobbing printer (perhaps he produced our football fixture-cards), and in his dusty office discovered the pleasures of selecting a typeface, paper, and ink (red for the cover, black for the text).

I told myself I would revise *King Lear* that afternoon, but must first persuade local bookshops to carry copies of *The Earthly Paradise* 'on sale or return'. No sooner had I sat down with the poor King after lunch, however, than a breathless messenger knocked on my door. There was a crisis in the kitchen. Would I (as President of the JCR) come at once? I found the college Chef being forcibly restrained by his under-chefs. He had just completed an icing-sugar model of the college to stand as centre-piece of the buffet at the Quincentenary Ball. It was a master-work, but someone had tactlessly called attention to a flaw. To make it more perfectly resemble the college on the night of the Ball, the Chef had installed electric lights to make the windows glow. 'But', said his critic, 'there are no lights in the *real* tower!'

The Chef was an artist with an artist's sensitivity to criticism and, seizing a rolling-pin, shouted that if his work was not appreciated he would destroy it. He was weeping when I arrived, but was persuaded to spare his creation on the understanding that I would ask the President of the college if life could imitate art; if there could be real lights in the real tower on the night of the Ball.

Returning to my room, I found that proofs of *The Earthly Paradise* had arrived and had a stronger claim on my attention than *King Lear* . . .

So much for the month of monastic seclusion. As our final exams approached, I decided on a high-risk strategy: for papers offering the candidate a choice of authors to be discussed, this candidate would prepare himself to answer questions only on poets – with one exception. In case the examiners supposed him unaware of the existence of the Novel, he would offer them his thoughts on Jane Austen.

The exams came and went and then the candidates went to bed for a week.

By ancient tradition, the Oxford academic year ends with Encaenia, the University's annual commemoration of founders and benefactors. This takes place in the baroque splendour of the Sheldonian Theatre, where the great and the good (and a good many who are neither) assemble in their finest feathers to hear an hour-long oration and the presentation of candidates for Honorary Degrees. The Public Orator and the Professor of Poetry take it in turns, year and year about, to deliver the oration. In 1958, it was Auden's turn to chronicle the events of that year – by medieval tradition, in Latin – and there was a pleasant irony in hearing the outgoing Public Orator's valediction 'spoken by one who, like the Pythian Priestess in her trance, utters he knows not what'.*

A later tradition was also still observed, by which the winner of the Newdigate Prize followed the orator into a gilded pulpit and recited an extract from his poem. Accordingly, on the morning of 25 June, I treated an audience impatient for lunch in All Souls to a slice of *Earthly Paradise*. 'At least it wasn't in Latin,' I heard someone say afterwards; and my own satisfaction was qualified by the knowledge that the printed copies available in bookshops all over Oxford were disfigured by a catastrophic misprint on the cover.

At least there were no misprints (of which I was aware) in the beribboned programme of the Magdalen Quincentenary Ball, two days later. Jill and I 'danced to the edge of the morning', but I wasn't good company. I had stewardly duties and, at the

---

* *at hodie devorandae sunt illi laudationis ineptiae ab homine pronuntiatae qui tamquam Pythia illa vates 'Phoebi nondum patiens' verbis delirat, quid ibi significetur prorsus ignorat.*

THE

EARTHLY PARADISE

By

Jon Stallworthy

not

' Then wilt thou be loath
To leave this Paradise, but shalt possess
A Paradise within thee, happier farr.'

PARADISE LOST, BK. XII, 585

The Newdigate Prize Poem

1958

Two Shillings and Sixpence net

back of my head, the first stirrings of what I took to be a Quincentenary Ode, but would later see as an elegy for a Magdalen 'life' dying as we danced.

★

Candidates for the Final Honours School of English, in the 1950s, were required to submit themselves to both a written exam and an oral inquisition. The latter, known as the *viva*, took place at the end of July and the results were announced at the start of August. It was thought desirable, in those few days, to put as many miles as possible between oneself and one's tutors and parents. Where then to go that was distant, beautiful, inexpensive, and invested with alluring literary associations? Three Magdalen friends – Dick Watson, Peter France, and I – decided the answer was Greece. We bought a copy of the *Blue Guide* and began to burrow in the small print of European train-timetables. Across these, however, lay the long shadow of the Inquisition.

On the morning of 30 July, I was interrogated by black-gowned Thought Police about answers someone of my name had allegedly given to questions of which I had no recollection. Twice I was asked to leave the room, and twice recalled. Going out finally for the third time seemed unpropitious, but I had no thought of omens as I stuffed Auden's *Poems* and Lawrence Durrell's *Bitter Lemons* into my rucksack and caught the London train.

By the time we reached Munich, where we were to join the *Deutschesstudentbundesring* train to Athens, our party had increased to seven with the addition of four more bolting under-graduates: two Bills, an Ed, and a Martin. In Munich, the four who had taken 'Finals' received the fateful telegrams that told Dick, Martin, and Peter they had 'Firsts'; I, that I had a 'Second'. I couldn't complain – I hadn't done enough work – and my dis-appointment was assuaged by a letter from Jill (opened before the telegram). I thought of her that night as I shook out my sleeping-bag on a clover-covered hilltop overlooked by moun-tains, itself overlooking Kochel am See.

Two nights later (my diary tells me), we filed into a darkened hay-loft like homing bees, and rhymes were humming in my head as I fell asleep. Clusters of words, transferred next morning from the back of my head to the back of my diary, formed them-selves into lines, which formed themselves into a stanza; and, for I think the first time, I became dimly aware of the poet's bifocal vision, regarding at once the ostensible subject of the poem and its musical structure. Over the next few days, they grew together in the train that, on 6 August, deposited us in Athens; its insistent rhythm no doubt contributing to that of the poem:*

Here and There

From a green sack on a green hill
Where the stars and clover meet,
I see the whiteness sheathing Jill;
Shadow-ripples on the sheet
From her little, brittle feet.

Clover heads nod in my face,
Whose purple and whose white suggest
That ribbon in the climbing lace
Upon the uplands of her breast;
The wind, her breathing from the west.

The mountains now contract their range,
The clouds – turned curtain – drift and fall
On stars beyond the arc of change.
Pines, church, and village shoulder all
Within a picture on the wall.

How should I pattern the soft dreams
That shade her pillow? May the bed
Outgrow the bedroom, singing streams
Flash from the walls above her head.
Carpet pastures round her spread.

The brimming mirror overflows
Into the oval of the lake;
And one reflection of a rose

* 'I think a railroad train a good place to write when the journey is long enough. One will exhaust the scenery in the first two or three hours and the newspaper in the second two or three hours (even an American newspaper), and towards the end of the day one can hardly help oneself, but one has begun to write. Indeed I think if some benevolent government would only shut one up in the smoking car of a railway train and send one across the world one would really write two or three dozen lyrics in the year.' W.B. Yeats to Lady Gregory, 21 January 1904.

Glitters in the moon's slow wake,
Until her dream and the day break.

Mountains surround her till the sun
Gild flower-pots on her window-sill.
Now let her climb the quilt, and run
Where the stars shoot and I lie still
In a green sack on a green hill.

Our first night in Athens we slept on the beach, until a distant hill ignited like a volcano, and a lava-wave of light washed us out of our sacks and into the sea. For three dazzling days we explored the city, then bussed to Delphi, and camped on a ledge overlooking the amphitheatre.

11 August [says my diary]: Awoke under pomegranates, & eagles spiralling around the cliffs with no visible movement of their wings. The sun does not scale the shoulder of Parnassus until 8. A quick run in the magnificent, empty, silent stadium – 'souls of runners dead & gone'. Below us, the temple & the olive valley came to light & life; bells tinkle faraway; birds sing all around us.

Peter, Ed & I go down to the Castalian spring: not the public trough by the road, but higher, under the overhang of the cliff, where the water runs laughing out of the hill: here the remains of wide steps, a broken pillar & a couple of niches in the stone face. We shave rapturously while on every side the Muses sit combing out their hair.

That afternoon, Dick and I climbed Parnassus, returning with pockets full of almonds picked up in the grass.

From Delphi, we went on to the monastery of Osios Loukas, the islands of Aegina and Poros, Epidauros, Nauplia, Argos, Mycenae, Corinth; camping for the most part on threshing floors like giant mill-stones, our sleeping-bags laid out in the pattern of a seven-pointed star.

Returning to Athens, the star broke up: Bill S. and Martin heading for Corfu; the rest of us catching the ferry to Mykonos.

We arrived after dark, slept on a headland, and woke (says the diary) on 27 August to find

> white horses racing in the bay, neighing underneath us, the two fishing-boats tugging & complaining at their cables, & at our backs – half-seen over the wall – the white sails of the windmill trotting round merrily. Boreas almost tugs us off our cliff as we dress & pack in an air of excitement & delight. We are late for breakfast, but cannot by-pass the windmill, or the donkey shaking its ears outside. I attempt to photograph the tightly-reefed canvas sails in their singing circuit: then inside the pepper-pot building, & up spiral stairs to where the great stones grind beneath churning home-carpentered cogs. The new flour trickles slowly, & as rich as cream, into its wooden box. Over this sits the miller on his stool: I look for his 'thumb of gold',* and he smiles serenely as the whirring machinery over his head threatens to carry away the roof like a helicopter. I should have liked to have squatted there all day, but breakfast calls. Peter buys the loaf out of the oven, & I the honey . . .

At 8.30, we boarded a fishing-boat that, bucking and rearing like an unbroken horse, carried us to the sacred island of Delos. Here the party divided again. After a morning in the Tourist Pavilion drinking lemonade to calm queasy stomachs, Bill G. and Ed caught the one-o'clock boat back to Mykonos. The Magdalen contingent, meanwhile, had seen enough of the island to know this was where we wanted to drop anchor. For three days, we searched the ruins for mosaics every morning – until the Swan Hellenic tourists came ashore from their liners – and again every afternoon when they had gone. In between, we read and swam in a sandy cove crossed by no footprints but our own. Every evening, we climbed the sacred mountain to watch the sunset; came down to meat-balls and ouzo in the Tourist Pavilion; and slept under a marble moon.

---

* Chaucer said of the Miller in his *Canterbury Tales* that 'he hadde a thombe of gold' (an ironic allusion to a proverb: 'An honest miller has a golden thumb').

Riding the Delos Lion: Jon, Peter, Dick

At the end of August, we sailed back to Athens and made one last literary pilgrimage. Passing Cape Sounion on the ferry, we had seen the Temple of Poseidon poised like a white wicker birdcage above an indigo sea. Now, approaching it from the land, we searched the names carved, scratched, and scribbled on its sixteen marble pillars for the object of our quest, and finally found it – **Byron** – elegantly incised with a winged **r** like a bird in flight. Tracing the name of the great Philhellene with my forefinger I felt no voltage, but it seemed a suitable gesture of farewell to

> The isles of Greece, the isles of Greece,
> Where burning Sappho loved and sung.

Six days, four countries, and a Channel crossing later, we reached our own island and – but perhaps the diary should have the last word:

10 minutes before the train goes: I phone Jill [at her flat in Ashburn Place]: her voice little & distant: she endorses the announcement that we will probably be late.

O intolerable train, dragging its slow length like a wounded snake along. We try to engross ourselves in the dark headlines of the Sunday papers: talk of the new hooking laws; of the power of the portrait photographer to bias all who see his pictures. Arabs show Nasser jovial and smiling, the English papers show him serpent-faced. Peter talks of Bill G's journal read in the train: a pronounced strain of melancholy, apparently. Strange how different journals will record the same event.

O intolerable train, will it *never* come to Victoria! 9 o'clock, 10 o'clock, 11 o'clock. I feel like a much-shaken champagne bottle. At last the station: then the taxi queue – O intolerable taxi-queue! Half past 11 however, sees me driven down the Cromwell Road. In the mounting excitement, Greece slips away, but I catch it for one second before it vanishes: think gratefully that the six weeks have given me an added field of reference, not to mention so many delights. There will be time later to recollect them all in tranquillity . . .

For the present – O intolerable taxi, why stop at all the traffic lights! But it came to Ashburn Place, & at last the cork could escape from the intolerable bottle!

7

Irish Manuscripts

MY MOTHER WAS a natural celebrant, always on the lookout for a reason to fill the house with flowers and declare a state of celebration. Few such causes pleased her more than a significant homecoming, for which she would prepare the homecomer's favourite meal, bring out her best china and linen napkins, light the candles, and, when everything was ready, ring her little brass bell.

My father, meanwhile, would have selected a Rather Special Bottle from his 'cellar' (a wine rack in the boot-room). It would, certainly, be Rather Special because, although he himself knew little and cared less about wine, many of his Grateful Patients knew a great deal and gave him something special in which to drink the health of a baby he had delivered. His Presbyterian upbringing – a teetotal grandfather had campaigned for Prohibition – had left him uneasy about alcohol, but he was a good host and liked to offer wine worthy of his Peggy's food.

I returned to Shotover Edge in September 1958 to find a state of celebration declared – in honour of my homecoming – and the kitchen fragrant with the smell of beef stew and dumplings. When the brass bell rang and we had taken our seats in front of the smoked salmon, my father said grace, as his father and grandfather had. Then, lifting his champagne glass, he proposed a toast to the baby whose birth had occasioned the bottle – 'the newcomer' – and then another to 'the homecomer' and his Degree.

I hadn't been looking forward to discussing my degree with him, since even 'a Good Second' (and in the days before second-class degrees were divided into 'Two-ones' and 'Two-twos', all Seconds were Good Seconds) was a far cry from his own 'Starred First'. I began a prepared apology, but he waved it aside and turned to a related topic about which I had also been feeling some unease – what I was going to do next – but this, it seemed, was decided: I was going to try again for a Blue.

'Third time lucky,' he said, and the family drank to that, too.

The problem was that, to stay up at university for a fourth year, a graduate student had to sign on for a graduate degree. I didn't want a graduate degree and had no intention of staying up beyond the end of that academic year. The problem had to be explained to the Chairman of the English Faculty Board, Miss Helen Gardner. She was then (and would long remain) Queen Bee of the Faculty hive, famous alike for her honey and her sting, and I approached her cell in Lady Margaret Hall with considerable anxiety – not least because, as one of my examiners, she would know the truth about my Good Second.

She glittered at me. 'So you've decided you want to do a graduate degree.'

'Not exactly, Miss Gardner.'

'What d'you mean: not exactly?'

'Well, I want to stay up –'

'– To do a graduate degree.'

'No, to play rugger.'

'You can play rugger *and* write a thesis.'

'But I'm not going to write a thesis.' Now for the sting, I thought. She'll tell me I'm wasting her time – as I was – but happily she was in a honeyed mood.

'Dear boy, I'm sure you can *begin* a thesis; whether or not you *finish* it is entirely up to you.' I felt we had reached a satisfactory understanding and could leave matters there, but Miss Gardner, I would learn, was not one to leave questions hanging in the air.

'Well, what are you going to work on?'

'I've no idea.'

'I suggest Yeats. You've probably seen *The Variorum Edition of the Poems* that's just been published. Fascinating variants. Have a look at them. Be good for *your* poems. I'll see if Maurice Bowra will supervise you.'

A few days later, I received a card '*From the Warden*, WADHAM COLLEGE', asking me to go and see him at 4.30 the following Monday. It was signed 'CMB'. I knew enough of Maurice Bowra's reputation to be at once intrigued and alarmed. I knew he was a scholar and a wit, and had laughed at the story of him towelling himself on the bank at Parson's Pleasure (a stretch of the river, to which women were not admitted, where men swam without bathing-suits) when a Peeping Thomasina was observed under a rug in a passing punt. The man beside him, wrapping his towel about his waist, was surprised to see the Warden wrap *his* about his head and, afterwards asking him why, was told: 'I like to think in Oxford it is by my face that I am known!'

When I knocked at the door of the Warden's Lodgings, it instantly flew open and my hand, which had not yet fallen to my side, was seized and briskly shaken by a shadowy figure who barked 'Come in, 'COME IN!' then hurried ahead of me into a sitting-room, where he waved me to an armchair and flopped into another. Prompted perhaps by a mental picture of the Warden naked on the river bank, it struck me that he looked like a benevolent bull-seal: huge head, top-heavy body (tightly encased in a grey suit) tapering to small feet, flippers extended on the arms of his chair.

'Glad you could come,' he said. 'After Monday meetings of the Hebdomadal Council, one needs intelligent conversation – and tea, China, of course.' (Only later would I understand that 'of course': Bowra had spent his childhood in China, where his father was an official in the Chinese Imperial Customs Service.)

He bent forward, lifted the teapot on the table between us, poured out two cups, and gave me one.

Maurice Bowra

'What is your college?'
'Magdalen.'
'So you know Tom Boase?'
'Yes.'
'Tom Boase, man of great public virtues but no private

parts.' Rattled by this conversational upper-cut, I could only sip my tea and try to stop the cup rattling in the saucer.

'But you didn't know Yeats?'

'No.'

'I did. Wrote me a poem, not a great poem, but a poem. I'd asked him to lunch, but he declined, unceremoniously. Misread my signature. Thought it was someone else – fearful shit – but discovered his mistake and was very contrite. Cared for ceremony, Yeats. Sent me this.' He picked up a copy of the *Collected Poems* that was lying beside the teapot, and read from the fly-leaf:

> To Maurice Bowra
>
> Sound words from Yeats to Bowra: he
> Asks pardon for stupidity
> Committed in the month of June,
> Hand laid on heart declares the moon
> The Almighty and Devil know
> What made a sane man blunder so.

That was the first – and worst – of many poems he would boom at me over the months that I sat at his flipper-feet, learning to read Yeats under a monologic fountain I would forever associate with a Yeatsian image:

> Homer had not sung
> Had he not found it certain beyond dreams
> That out of life's own self-delight had sprung
> The abounding glittering jet . . .

Every Monday afternoon, I would arrive at 4.30 with my copy of Yeats's *Variorum Poems* and a notebook. While Bowra performed the tea ceremony, I would report the findings from my reading the previous week – a pattern in the post-publication revisions of, let's say, Yeats's 1921 collection, *Michael Robartes and the Dancer*. Then the fountain would start playing an encouraging overture. My comments were 'VERY INTERESTING', he would say, rephrasing, relaunching them so that they sparkled in the air. Then would come questions, some easy ones to which I could reply, followed by a sudden jet from a different angle.

'Has it struck you how Yeats's poems about the Easter Rising resemble Blok's about the Russian Revolution?'

'Blocks?'

'Blok, Blok, you know Blok!'

'I don't think I do.'

He flippered out of his chair and out of the room. I heard him patter up the stairs and, after a moment or two of astonishing silence, patter down again. He reappeared, book in hand, filling the room with the sibillant blizzard of Alexander Blok's great poem, 'The Twelve'. A banner was flapping in the wind across the St Petersburg street. He translated its dancing Cyrillic: 'ALL POWER TO THE CONSTITUENT ASSEMBLY'. An old woman appears. She eyes it, thinking 'How many children's leggings it would make'. Other figures appear: a writer, a fat priest, a smart lady, prostitutes, and then the twelve Red Guards. I heard their voices – in Russian, and then in English. Together, we relived Blok's revolutionary night.

'And when it was finished,' said Bowra, 'he wrote in his notebook: "Today I am a genius."' I didn't doubt Blok was right, and emerging into the Oxford night – our conversations always ended at 7 o'clock, when the Warden dressed for dinner – I hurried to the Bodleian and ordered up his book *The Heritage of Symbolism*, and all the translations of 'The Twelve' that I could find in the catalogue.

Returning to read them next day, I was disappointed. It was as if, having gone in search of a great animal, I could find only its skeleton – a great skeleton, certainly, but draped in a dead language with none of the muscular music I remembered.

> The mad wind hurts,
> Is mad and gay;

It blows the skirts,
Mows the passers-by,
Shakes, quakes and makes fly
The great placard away:
'All power to the Constituent Assembly.'

This and other of Bowra's translations in *The Heritage of Symbolism* had none of the vitality of his spoken rendering. Cyril Connolly called him a poet *manqué*, and his conversation was all that one expects of a poet (and rarely finds), but he was no poet on the page. My disappointment, however, was soon succeeded by a wild and happy thought. I would try to translate Blok myself. The following Monday, I nervously asked Bowra what he thought of the idea. 'Excellent, EXCELLENT!' he said, and put me in touch with Max Hayward, then the leading British translator from the Russian, with whom in due course I translated 'The Twelve'.

Max was what the Irish call 'a darling man', genial, generous, and a natural teacher. He had the stocky good looks of a Second World War Yugoslav partisan, and an east European passion for alcohol and poetry. Doctors had persuaded him to forego the first, but only an early death would disengage him from the second. He taught me that translating a great poet is a form of master-class more demanding and more rewarding than critical analysis.

Max would give me a literal line-by-line prose version of a poem, with an approximate metrical score (above the words), notes on rhyme and rhythm, tone, vocabulary, repetitions, ambiguities of meaning, and so on. This prose version I would then try to coax into the diction and rhythms of a twentieth-century English poem, with as little alteration as possible. Assuming that the general movement and tone of the English poem were a fair reflection of the Russian (which wasn't always the case), Max would offer specific criticisms and I would try again. Our dialogue would continue for several exchanges, interspersed with readings from the Russian to give me a better idea of the sound I was striving for. We made things difficult for ourselves by trying to reproduce the metrical form of the original, or an appropriate English equivalent; believing that to translate a metrical poem into free verse was to translate an oil painting into a black–and–white photograph. Did our colour photograph of 'The Twelve' do justice to Blok's masterpiece? More, we liked to think, than any previous photograph, but no one knew better than we did the inadequacies of our celluloid copy. For me, however, our failure was more than outweighed by what Blok and Hayward taught me about the architectonics of poetic structure and the density of poetic language.

The ripples from Bowra's beneficent fountain didn't stop with Blok and Hayward, but extended into my own poems. (*A Familiar Tree* would have been impossible but for the polyphonic example of 'The Twelve'.) And on other Mondays, 'The abounding glittering jet' threw up the poems of Pasternak (which I would later translate with Peter France), Cavafy, Seferis, Quasimodo, and dozens of other names new to me, names scribbled in my notebook, later to be looked up in the Bodleian catalogue.

*

The hours I spent in the library, under the glazed gaze of Addison, Dryden, and Waller, were fewer than those spent at the Iffley Road rugger ground. I was training hard. At 5 foot 9 and 11 stone, slighter and lighter than most club rugby forwards, I had to be fitter than the others if I was to hold my own. My sense that the omens were good, however, seemed to be confirmed when the new captain of the OURFC, Theo Lombard, asked me to play for his team against the Oxford Club, traditionally the opening match of the University season. On paper it was a strong team: I was hooking between two Blues, Lombard and Jesson, and there were five others in the side, three of them

Internationals. We won 11–0, but as *The Times* reported next day: 'Lombard's forwards were poor and there is a lot of work to be done before they can become a satisfactory pack. In this game they were outplayed.' A week later was the OURFC Final Trial and again I was hooking for the Blue side, this time against a formidable Freshman, Dil Davies, who had already played for Aberavon. He was larger and heavier than me, but I scored a try and was dashed at half-time to be asked to swop jerseys with him. 'In hooking there wasn't much to choose between Stallworthy and Davies,' said *The Times*. The writing was on the wall, and the following week the writing on the match-card for the University against Leicester had D.M. Davies between D. Jesson and L.T. Lombard.

I didn't lose hope that the writing might be revised and, together with other hopefuls, set my sights on the Greyhounds' fourth-week match against the University, remembering how David had overthrown Goliath two years before. The Greyhounds won their first two matches – the second, against the United Services at Chatham, by 25–5 – and there was a fine pre-Agincourt spirit in our changing-room when, at overlong last, the Wednesday of the fourth week arrived and 'like grey-hounds in the slips,/Straining upon the start', we waited to take the field. It was Guy Fawkes Day and raining, which suited us well. We hoped it might douse the rockets on the other side, particularly John Young, the fastest wing-three-quarter in England.

As the *Manchester Guardian* reported the battle that followed:

> [The University] scraped home by a somewhat lucky try to nothing in a hard but undistinguished game and had very much the worse of things in the second half. With a little more speed and safety in hand-ling, the Greyhounds could have scored a deserved victory. . . . The University pack was completely outplayed in the second half.

One member of the Greyhound pack was promoted, but it wasn't the hooker. He was disappointed but, surprisingly soon, found himself entrenched as happily as ever in the Greyhound front line; indeed, more happily than ever, since this was a better team than those of 1956 and 1957. It was better because better balanced, with no 'stars' and no weak links; fifteen companionable enthusiasts with one objective – to beat the Cambridge LX Club on 4 December. We trained together every weekday afternoon, other than days when there were matches, and every match we won.

The clashing of heads as each pair of front rows packed down, wrestling for the supremacy that would win their 'backs' the ball, had turned my shell-like ears to cauliflowers. Every Saturday night they would be suffused with blood, and every Monday I would have them lanced and drained in hospital before presenting myself at Wadham.

The LX Club match was to be held in Cambridge and, on the day, the sun turned out to watch us play our last game together. History (in the person of the *Manchester Guardian* reporter) would say:

> It took the Cambridge University LX Club almost forty minutes to reach the Oxford University Greyhounds' 25[-yard line]. . . . Oxford, on the other hand, rarely relaxed control of the game and looked capable of scoring more than their four tries. But with an advantage from line-outs, set scrums, and loose scrums, they all too often threw wild passes when near the line or outran their supporting wings . . .

I remember it, less soberly, as a carnival. Confident that we couldn't lose, we tried all the moves we had planned and practised: 'scissors' and 'dummy scissors'; cunning kicks; our scrum-half launching himself left in the familiar swallow-dive (but without the ball in his hands), drawing the defenders while, unnoticed on the other side of the field, a wing (ball under arm) sprinted for the line. But History tells the truth: we made mistakes. We were taking risks joyfully and with a wild exhilaration that mounted as the minutes ticked by on the referee's watch.

All too soon it was over and, back in a steamy changing-room,

we shared the perfect happiness of climbers at the top of a mountain. In that moment, I knew I could never be so fit or play so
well again. I knew I should enjoy watching rugger for the rest of
my life and, if I was lucky, teaching a son to play; but I also knew
– and the knowledge in no way diminished the happiness – that
I should never play again. And I never did.

★

Coming down from a mountain is harder than climbing it, especially when one has climbed it as a member of a team and comes
down on one's own. Returning, after Christmas, to the high
room in Holywell Street that I was renting from a friend of my
mother, I missed the company of the *comitatus*, the fellowship of
the scrum, afternoons at Iffley Road, evenings talking tactics at
the King's Arms. The company of my fellow graduates on the
B.Litt. course, talking of theses and college lectureships, was a
poor exchange. I felt a fraud. They were going to be dons, I was
not, having accepted the offer of an editorial job with the
Oxford University Press from the following October. In the
meantime, as a B.Litt. candidate, I was committed to attend
classes on hand-printing and palaeography, designed for embryo
scholars of Renaissance literature long before the Oxford
English Faculty had dreamt of admitting embryo scholars of
Modern literature. I didn't see how a mastery of the mysteries
of hand-printing or Renaissance handwriting could conceivably
be of help or relevance to a twentieth-century publisher, but
having signed up for those classes, I duly attended and found
them, it must be said, more amusing than I had expected.

Much more amusing, however, and much more relevant to
my real ambitions were still the Monday afternoons in Wadham.
Now that I was no longer distracted by what Bowra called my
'gladiatorial aspirations', I could give more time to Yeats. The
Irish Archpoet had dedicated his autobiographical *Reveries over
Childhood and Youth*:

TO
THOSE FEW PEOPLE
MAINLY PERSONAL FRIENDS
WHO HAVE READ
ALL THAT I HAVE WRITTEN

and his friend, the Warden, suggested I should do the same. The previous Christmas, Geoffrey Keynes had given me a copy of Allan Wade's *Bibliography of the Writings of W.B. Yeats* and, setting myself to read in chronological order everything this listed, there soon landed on my' desk in the Bodleian a plum-coloured *Poems of Spenser*, 'Selected and with an Introduction by W. B. Yeats', published in 1906. The Introduction was a revelation. It told me:

Like an hysterical patient [Spenser] drew a complicated web of inhuman logic out of the bowels of an insufficient premise – there was no right, no law, but that of Elizabeth, and all that opposed her opposed themselves to God, to civilisation, and to all inherited wisdom and courtesy, and should be put to death. . . . When Spenser wrote of Ireland he wrote as an official, and out of thoughts and emotions that had been organised by the State. He was the first of many Englishmen to see nothing but what he was desired to see. . . . He is 'sure it is yet a most beautiful and sweet country as any is under heaven,' and that all would prosper but for those agitators, those 'wandering companies that keep the wood,' and he would rid it of them by a certain expeditious way. There should be four great garrisons, 'And those fowre garrisons issuing foorthe, at such convenient times as they shall have intelligence or espiall upon the enemye, will so drive him from one side to another, and tennis him amongst them, he shall finde nowhere safe to keepe his creete [cattle], or hide himselfe, but flying from the fire shall fall into the water, and out of one daunger into another, that in short space his creete, which is his moste sustenaunce, shall be wasted in preying, or killed in driving, or starved for wante of pasture in the woodes, and he himselfe brought soe lowe, that he shall have no harte nor abilitye to indure his wretchednesse, the which will surely come to passe in very short space; for one winters well following of him will soe plucke him on his knees that he will never be able to stand up agayne.'

He could commend this expeditious way from personal knowl-edge, and could assure the Queen that the people of the country would soon 'consume themselves and devoure one another. The proofs whereof I saw sufficiently ensampled in these late warres in Mounster; for notwithstanding that the same was a most rich and plentifull countrey, full of corne and cattell, that you would have thought they would have bene able to stand long, yet ere one yeare and halfe they were brought to such wretchednesse, as that any stonye harte would have rued the same. Out of every corner of the woodes and glynnes they came creeping forth upon theyr hands, for theyr legges could not beare them; they looked like anatomyes of death, they spake like ghostes crying out of theyr graves; they did eate of the dead carrions, happy were they if they could finde them, yea, and one another soone after, insoemuch as the very carcasses they spared not to scrape out of theyr graves; and if they found a plot of water-cresses or shamrokes, there they flocked as to a feast for the time, yet not able long to continue therewithall; that in short space there were none allmost left, and a most populous and plentifull countrey sud-daynely made voyde of man or beast; yet sure in all that warre, there perished not many by the sword, but all by the extremitye of famine.'

This quotation led me to its source, Spenser's *View of the Present State of Ireland*, which gave me a new view of the *Pax Britannica*.

Yeats's Introduction went on to speak of 'the accursed house of Cromwell', reminding me of one of his late poems, 'The Curse of Cromwell', which I had evidently not understood:

You ask what I have found and far and wide I go:
Nothing but Cromwell's house and Cromwell's murderous crew,
The lovers and the dancers are beaten into the clay,
And the tall men and the swordsmen and the horsemen where
    are they?

My knowledge of history was derived in the main from litera-ture. I knew that Andrew Marvell had written an encomiastic

'Horatian Ode upon Cromwell's Return from Ireland', but no
one had told me – nor had I thought to ask – why he went or
what he had done there. When I discovered, it set me reading
about the Maori Wars in New Zealand and wondering what life
had been like in England under the Romans.

★

My own life was still centred on Yeats (from Monday to Friday)
and Jill (from Friday to Sunday). At weekends we still picnic'd by
the Windrush or punted on the Cherwell with Richard and
Kate, who were now married and living – appropriately – in
Paradise Street. Jill and I talked of marriage, 'but not yet'. I had
to have a job and a salary, and she wanted to see something of
the world beyond Oxford and London. She had worked for *The
Economist* for five years, and since the Queen hadn't paid her to
go abroad on National Service, sensibly decided to pay her own
way – to Capri, for four months as an *au pair* in a princely household. It didn't seem sensible to me, and the prospect of her
departure began to darken my days and poems:

> Walking – but you not with me – round
> a glass sky fallen into Blenheim lake,
> I see the wind's invisible dancers waltz
> from hill to water, and the cloud-floes break
> superbly into swans. And I
> who know what songs the fields are singing, drowned
> in their green wave, know that the singers lie.
> The rooks trumpet for summer on a false
> alarm. Else why should you, my swan,
> be restless to move on?

Jill left at the start of June, and to counter my self-pitying
gloom, I returned to physical exercise. The annual University
Punt Race against Cambridge was to be held there in a fortnight's time, and I did well enough in the trials to be chosen for

the eight-man – and one woman – relay team. The woman, Celia Blaze, was our 'baton' and on the day of the race, dressed as a Dresden shepherdess, took up her position in the bow of the first Oxford punt. It was a glorious day, and the college lawns leading down to the Cam were thronged with a crowd as colourful as a Seurat canvas. Our captain had won the toss and chosen the Huntingdonshire side of the river, 'a terrible mistake as any Cambridge men could have told [him],' said the *Manchester Guardian* next day, 'because it meant a muddy bottom all the way'.

This we discovered when the starting-pistol cracked and the two punts, side by side, surged from the shadow of St John's Bridge. While the Cambridge pole came away cleanly from gravel at the end of every thrust, Oxford's had to be tugged from partisan mud. At the end of the first 'leg', Cambridge were leading by two lengths, a lead they increased at the turn. Their 'baton' was wearing jeans and leaped into their second boat like a greyhound, while Celia parachuted into ours with a billowing of petticoats, at which

> All Rome sent forth a rapturous cry,
> And even the ranks of Tuscany
> Could scarce forbear to cheer.

As our second boat covered the course in the reverse direction, the puntsman's pole was plucked from his hands by Cambridge spectators on one of the bridges and, although it was returned to him, its seizure cost him another yard or two. I was to punt the last-but-one lap and, by the time the billowing baton reached me, we were many lengths behind, but then my opponent lost his pole and, with it, much of his lead. He finished only a few yards ahead and, as the anchormen found their rhythm on the home straight, it seemed that ours might overhaul theirs. At this point, however, the god of the Cam – Milton's 'Camus, reverend sire' – intervened. The Oxford pole snapped, and the Cambridge punt crossed the finishing line first. The afternoon

ended, like a scene from *Zuleika Dobson*, with everyone throw-
ing themselves into the river.

★

At what Maurice Bowra called 'our last séance', he asked me if
I had thought of going over to Dublin to see Mrs Yeats.

'What for?' I said. 'I'm not going to write a thesis.'

'You would like her, dear boy, and she might like you.
Remember *The Aspern Papers*.'

So I wrote to Mrs Yeats, asking if I could see her husband's
manuscripts, and while waiting for an answer, went camping
with Geoffrey Keynes. He was now 72 and, having found 'the
perfect camp-site', was anxious to share it with his friends. This
was in the park of Felbrigg House, a few miles inland from
Cromer. Geoffrey thought 'Felbrigg with its unique Italianate
façade of about 1600 . . . the most lovely of all the Stately Homes
of Norfolk'. It was owned by his friend, Wyndham Ketton-
Cremer, whose family had lived there for four and a half cen-
turies. He hadn't expected to inherit it, but did so on the death
of an elder brother in the battle for Crete.

Wyndham was a bachelor in his fifties and, temperamentally,
a scholar rather than a landowner. He had written biographies
of Thomas Gray and Horace Walpole and, when I met him that
first evening, seemed to me like one of the Strawberry Hill circle
himself: an eighteenth-century country gentleman with antiquarian and botanical tastes and hypochondriac tendencies. As
the septuagenarian sipped his sherry and enthused about the
clearing in which we had set up our tent, Wyndham became agi-
tated at the thought of the rain that could drench us, the wind
off the North Sea that could chill us, the *lightning* . . .! Should he
not ask his man to make up beds for us in the house? No? Then
he really must insist that we allow him to give us a hot supper
one evening. That was agreed, and we were about to head for
our gypsy meal over an open fire when we were happily dis-

214

Felbrigg: the west and south fronts

tracted. Beyond the great bay window of Wyndham's study lay
a broad sweep of grassland and, as we watched, seven shepherds
and their dogs came up over the skyline. It was a vision of
another England.

I woke next morning – as I would wake every morning
during our week at Felbrigg – to sunshine and the shadow-play
of leaves on sloping canvas, and a chorus of wood-pigeons.
While Geoffrey resuscitated the fire, I walked up to the house
for a bucket of water and a small churn of milk. Then, after
breakfast, we would set off in Geoffrey's Rover for a favourite
church ('Remarkable glass and brasses') or an antiquarian bookshop ('Found an inscribed Gibbon there last year'). And every
afternoon, the hunt would end on the wide beaches at
Holkham. Swimming there, I thought of Badagry and Hazel,
then of Capri and Jill, and was silent on the drive back to camp.

Our dinner at Felbrigg came at the end of such a day. Wearing
ties and jackets for the first time that week, we walked up to the
house, entered by the tradesman's door, and passed through a
boot-room in which sixteen pairs of shoes were waiting for the
duster. Wyndham's man, Ward ('You must call him *Mr* Ward,'

Geoffrey had told me), led us back into the eighteenth century. We took Madeira in the Library, its dark shelves topped with Gothic pinnacles, before going down to dinner where Wyndham spoke of Gray and Walpole as if, at any moment, their carriages might draw up at the great door on the south front. After dessert, we moved out to the west lawn and – as our host urgently recommended – kept the dangerous night chill at bay with coffee and brandy. The barley-sugar trunks of a screen of sweet chestnuts gradually faded from sight at the end of the lawn. A new moon rose over their dark heads. Bats were cutting arabesques above our own. Then Wyndham shivered, and it was time for bed.

★

When I got back to Oxford, there was no letter waiting for me from Mrs Yeats.

'Don't worry, just go,' said Maurice Bowra, 'and if you need any help, ask the Librarian of Trinity. Dr O'Neill. Student of mine.'

'Don't worry, just go,' said my father, 'and if you need any help, ask Bethel Solomons, Dublin's leading gynaecologist.' He gave me his phone number and told me a story (told him by the man himself). Bethel Solomons had, in his youth, been an international rugger player. Once, taking a taxi home after a match in which Ireland had been trounced by England, he said to the driver:

'Did you see the game?' By way of answer, the taxi-driver spat out of the window.

'You didn't think much of the Irish team?'

'D'ye call that an *Irish* team?' said the taxi-driver. 'Fourteen Protestants and one bloody Jew?'

'You'd like Bethel,' my father said. I thought I probably should, but didn't expect to need the help of a gynaecologist.

I flew to Dublin in early June, booked a room in the cheapest guest-house I could find, and rang Mrs Yeats's phone number. There was no reply. I rang again and again the next day, and still there was no reply. Finally, in desperation, I rang Bethel Solomons and explained my predicament. Did he know where she might be?

'She's surely at home.'

'Then she's not answering her phone.'

'Ah no, but if you'll come round for a drink, we'll raise her.' This seemed to promise a magical invocation and, certainly, the face that came to Bethel Solomons' door could have been that of a benevolent magician: a wise and handsome face dominated, like that of Robert Graves, by a 'Crookedly broken nose – low tackling caused it'. There were laughter lines about the eyes and mouth.

'Come in, come in,' he said and, with a necromantic flourish, poured a generous libation of gin and a less generous libation of tonic into two tall glasses, one of which he gave me.

'To poetry,' he said. We touched glasses and drank. Then, going to the phone, he dialled a number and laid the receiver on the table without putting it to his ear.

'You know Mrs Yeats?' I said.

'Indeed. Didn't I deliver her children?'

'So you knew the poet, too?'

'*Knew* him? I rented him the flat over my consulting rooms in Merrion Square. He painted the sitting-room black – as an aid to inspiration.'

Easing himself out of his chair, he went over to the phone, put the receiver to his ear, returned it to the table top, and sat down again; a procedure repeated two or three times over the next five or ten minutes, until finally there was a voice at the other end of the line.

'George?' he said. 'It's Bethel, and I've a young poet here, who's been working on W.B. and would like to meet you. Can I send him round? . . . Right. Tomorrow, 11 o'clock?' He looked at me, raising an interrogative eyebrow, and I nodded vigorously.

'Yes, that's fine. And you're well?' Her reply made him laugh, and he put the phone down.

'How did you know she was there?' I asked.

'Ah well, I've known her long enough to know she doesn't answer the phone until it suits her; just as she doesn't open a letter unless she recognizes the writing or the typewriter. It saves her being bothered by Americans who want her to write their theses for them, or by the Inland Revenue.'

'She doesn't open letters from the Inland Revenue?'

'Never.'

'And they don't prosecute her?'

'This is Ireland. How could they prosecute the wife of the Archpoet? No. Your man from the Inland Revenue has a quiet word with her bank manager and they work out something between them.'

Walking back to my guest-house, I remembered that Edmund Spenser, the British civil servant, had deplored the Irish poets' power over the people, and that three of the fifteen executed leaders of the 1916 Easter Rising had been poets. If, in 1958, even the Irish Civil Service deferred to the power of poetry, Ireland, I decided, was a country after my own heart.

*

At 11 o'clock next morning, I climbed the steps of a red-brick house in the Rathmines suburb of Dublin and rang the bell. In the long silence that followed, I would have turned away had I not known Mrs Yeats's tactics. At last, I heard a shuffling and the drawing of a bolt. The door opened a wary inch. No face met mine, however, until looking down I made out two bright eyes under the brim of a dark felt hat. I explained who I was. The eyes did not blink nor the door move. I began again: 'Bethel Solomons . . .', and as if I had said 'Open Sesame', the door swung inward and I was admitted.

Mrs Yeats was not yet 70, but twenty-one years of marriage –

to a man twice her age on their wedding-day – and nineteen years of widowhood had taken their toll and she looked 80. Not that I had a clear impression of the old lady who led me from the dark passage into the sunlit study. I was too busy identifying the portraits thronging her walls – Yeats at all ages, Synge, Lady Gregory – and, on the mantelpiece, the exquisitely carved dwarf mountain that gave birth to the great late poem, 'Lapis Lazuli':

> Every discolouration of the stone,
> Every accidental crack or dent
> Seems a water-course or an avalanche,
> Or lofty slope where it still snows
> Though doubtless plum or cherry-branch
> Sweetens the little half-way house
> Those Chinamen climb towards, and I
> Delight to imagine them seated there;
> There, on the mountain and the sky,
> On all the tragic scene they stare.
> One asks for mournful melodies;
> Accomplished fingers begin to play.
> Their eyes mid many wrinkles, their eyes,
> Their ancient, glittering eyes, are gay.

Those weren't the only ancient glittering eyes in the room.

'Won't you sit there?' said Mrs Yeats, and I settled myself in the high-backed chair, at the right of the window, to which she pointed. She herself sat in a similar chair on the other side of the window, and began to ask me questions in a cultivated English voice (I had forgotten she was English). Remembering *The Aspern Papers*, I remembered that *I* should be questioning *her*, but there were difficulties: for one thing, I couldn't *see* her – the sun was full in my face – and, for another, some of her questions, so mildly delivered, had a wicked spin on them. It dawned on me that, far from interviewing the Archpoet's relict, I was myself being subjected to a skilful interrogation. I explained that my study of her husband's revisions, set out in *The Variorum Edition*

of the Poems, and the few manuscripts I had seen quoted in the
critical literature, suggested that he tended to reduce the personal
element in the successive stages of a poem's composition; and
I wondered whether a study of the manuscripts would confirm
(or disprove) this hypothesis.

'You want to see the manuscripts?'

'I was hoping I might see some of them.'

'Do you have particular poems in mind?'

'Yes, I have a list.' I handed it to her and shaded my eyes so
that I could watch her read it. Her face showed nothing of what
she was thinking.

'Excuse me,' she said and left the room. Nervously, I continued my examination of her pictures until – after what seemed
an eternity – she returned. She was carrying half a dozen notebooks.

'I think you'll find these interesting,' she said. 'Where do
you propose to work on them?'

'I have an introduction to the Librarian of Trinity College.'

'Very good. You can use my telephone to make an appointment to see him.' I rang his secretary, who said he was free at 2.30
that afternoon.

She was not at her desk when I arrived, but sharp at 2.30, I
knocked at the Librarian's door. A voice said 'Come in,' and I did
so, holding the notebooks in front of me like the Crown Jewels.

'Who the hell are you?' roared the little man behind the
large desk. I told him who I was and why I was there, adding:
'Sir Maurice Bowra asked me to give you his greetings.'

'I don't care if he did. You can't just come barging in like
this.'

'But your secretary . . .' I stammered.

'Get out!' he said.

Half an hour later, I was back in Rathmines trying to explain
my expulsion to Mrs Yeats.

'Will you ring for a taxi?' she said. 'We'll go to the National
Library in Kildare Street.' Arriving there, she asked if she could

see Mr Alf MacLochlainn. He received us very affably, gave us a cup of tea and, when she asked if I could read the notebooks there, said 'Of course.' It was agreed I would start the following morning and, just as we were about to leave, she said: 'Oh, and one more thing, Mr MacLochlainn. I've decided to leave my manuscripts to the National Library.'

'What can I say?' he asked.

'No need to say anything,' she said, and he didn't. His face said it all: astonishment, delight, and gratitude.

I thought I should like to see the Librarian of Trinity's face when he heard the news.

★

Exhausted by the roller-coaster ride from delight to despair and back again, I went to bed that night grateful I shouldn't have to travel that route next day. Tomorrow, the high plateau. The notebooks – *my* notebooks – were waiting to induct me into the secret life of Yeats's poems.

I reached the library early, and was the first to take a seat in the Manuscript Room. An assistant brought me a tin box – *my* treasure-chest – out of which I lifted the first notebook, and opened it at the first page. It was dense with dark writing, and I couldn't read one word. The second was the same, and the third, and the fourth. I turned the pages faster and faster. Unable to read anything in that notebook, I lifted the second out of the tin with the same result; and the third, and the fourth, and the fifth, and the sixth. Two hours had passed and I hadn't read one word.

I went out for a cup of coffee and found my hands were shaking. 'This is silly,' I told myself. 'Start again and take it slowly.' I did so, but at lunchtime the score was the same. I bought myself a sandwich and a magnifying glass, but when the library closed for the day I was still staring at pages as impenetrable as Dead Sea scrolls.

Supper in the guest-house was dispiriting at the best of times,

and worse at the worst of times. Eating my cold cabbage among
the living dead – desolate geriatrics abandoned by the world – I
had almost decided to abandon my quest, when I remembered
the Oxford palaeography class. Renaissance handwriting had
been as impenetrable to me, initially, as Yeats's. Studying the
letter-forms, however, and working out which 'ascender'
belonged to a *b*, which to a *d*, which 'descender' to a *j*, which to
a *y*, one began to recognize letters, and then words. I would
apply the same method to Yeats's barbarous scrawl.

It didn't work; or not until the second (or was it the third?)
day of that nightmare week, when a series of squiggles suddenly
called to mind a phrase from one of the poems. If that intuition
was correct – if this squiggle was an uncrossed *t* and that an
undotted *i* – and if the 'words' above and below were from a draft
of the same poem, then this could be . . . and it was. Slowly I
decoded the page, and the next, and the next; not every word,
for in Yeats's shorthand the word 'then', for example, can be
indistinguishable from 'there', 'their', 'the', 'this', 'these', or
'those'; but I was soon decoding enough to know whether a particular page was relevant to my quest. And none of them were.

When I took the notebooks back to Mrs Yeats, I had to tell
her that none of the poems I wanted were there.

'Ah no,' she said, 'but I thought you'd find them interesting.'
(As in a fairy-tale 'test', she had given me the six most difficult
notebooks.) 'Remind me again of the poems you wanted.'

Again I gave her my list and again she left the room. She
returned with a bundle of brown envelopes, which I took back
to the National Library and found to contain what was to me
pure gold: the manuscripts of one great poem after another. But
not always *all* the manuscripts. On one of my increasingly frequent visits to her house, I said: 'I don't believe this.'

'What don't you believe?'

'That this envelope contains all the manuscripts of "Sailing
to Byzantium".'

'Why not?'

First manuscript draft of the first stanza of 'Byzantium' by W.B. Yeats

'I don't believe that there are rough drafts of stanzas two, three, and four, but not of stanza one. This envelope suggests that work on stanza one began with a corrected typescript of the complete poem. I don't believe it.'

Mrs Yeats said nothing, but left the room, returning shortly with another brown envelope.

'Is this what you want?' It contained four manuscript folios.

'Thank you, yes.'

★

At weekends, when the Library was closed, I explored the broad streets and back-alleys of Yeats's city, the city of Swift and Joyce and Synge and O'Casey. The General Post Office I already knew from frequent visits to its *poste restante* counter, in the hope of finding a fat letter with an Italian stamp. It had been extensively rebuilt after the siege of Easter 1916, and the rising and the falling commemorated by a bronze statue of the dying hero, Cuchulain, as by Yeats's 'Statues' (*monumentum aere perennius*):

> When Pearse summoned Cuchulain to his side,
> What stalked through the Post Office?

I walked the Quays, imagining gunboats on the Liffey, manoeuvring into position to shell the GPO and other buildings held by the insurgents. I visited the site of the old Abbey Theatre (burnt down in 1951) and obeyed the imperatives of Yeats's poem, 'The Municipal Gallery Revisited':

> You that would judge me do not judge alone
> This book or that, come to this hallowed place
> Where my friends' portraits hang and look thereon;
> Ireland's history in their lineaments trace;
> Think where man's glory most begins and ends
> And say my glory was I had such friends.

Every evening, after fortifying myself with a glass or two of Guinness, I would return to supper in the guest-house. Perhaps because I was lonely, I became more aware of the loneliness of others – one old woman, in particular, who took her place in a poem that came to me one night as I walked the dark streets before bed:

Still Life

A feature of the guest-house window
like the cracked pane and the shrivelled fly,
she drops no stitches if the lap-dogs bark
nor flinches when a bus throbs by.
She who is nobody's wife or widow
sits, like a furled umbrella from the hall,
watching the boys play cricket in the park
and powerless to retrieve their ball.

With a knitting-needle quill all day
she writes the latest chapter of her life
for grandchildren, not hers, to stretch and pull,
rough-handle till it fray. They would not laugh
at the loose hand so readily, if they
could read the breaking heart between the lines.
Pity and terror fit her parable
for the grey language of the skeins.

She does not, like the house-maid, hear the clock
have hourly palpitations on the wall.
She does not hear the chauffeur's double knock
and the jolt of the chest in the hall.
Through the cracked window-pane leaks in the dark
until it seems she scarcely breathes at all;
watching the boys play cricket in the park
and powerless to retrieve their ball.

I was quite pleased with this. It seemed to me to owe nothing to Dylan Thomas or Yeats. I see now that it did: my feeling for the subject of my Still Life (I liked the multiple meanings of the title) surely owed something to my feelings for Mrs Yeats – not that she sat in her window knitting or, so far as I could judge, suffered from a breaking heart. The 'writing' metaphor, however, behind 'the loose hand' and 'between the lines' – a phrase I would later take as the title of my book on the making of Yeats's poetry – can only have derived from the hand and the lines to which I returned on Monday mornings.

.
★

I was now ordering and transcribing the manuscripts of poem after poem, and spending an increasing amount of time in Mrs Yeats's basement kitchen where, side by side at the scrubbed table, we would puzzle out difficult readings, passing the magnifying glass from hand to hand. I saw her no longer as an alarming figure from *The Aspern Papers*, defending her poet's literary remains and reputation from the defiling hands of 'publishing scoundrels' (like myself), but as a Fairy Godmother. She measured out my afternoons with pots of tea and answered my endless questions, often spicing her answer with a good story: as – to illustrate her husband's lifelong inability to punctuate properly – of the time when she was taking down a prose passage at his dictation and, after three-quarters of an hour, he suddenly said, ·'Comma'.

The fascination of Yeats's manuscripts is that they offer a graphic record of his voice in the act of composition, a record more complete than that of any other major poet in the English language. Where others compose extended passages in their heads and then write them down, Yeats would often scribble a prose draft of his initial idea and, it would seem, almost every word of the development that followed. Mrs Yeats confirmed the evidence of his execrable handwriting that, as he grew older, he frequently wrote with no intention of reading what was before him on the page. Like a locksmith opening a safe, he was searching for the right combination and, as the dials turned slowly beneath his fingers, his trained ear listened for the click of cogs slipping into place. One by one the numbers would come up, until finally the door swung open on a completed poem. He was in fact *thinking* on paper, and following the track of his pen or pencil, one seems to be at his elbow with the great voice chanting in one's ear.

As in a master-class, I saw and heard him building his musical structures and saw – what I had always sensed – that it is its musical structure that distinguishes poetry from prose. I learned how he balanced a sentence and built it into a stanza, and how sentence and stanza and poem were undergirded with rhetoric deployed like a sculptor's armature. I learned how he softened the outlines of his rhetorical framework, and freed his rhythms, as a poem took shape; concealing his artifice until the words on the page might pass for natural speech. I saw, in the unfolding of his career, the development of a fierce self-critical faculty that would strike out a line – even at times a stanza – better than anything I would ever write, because it was *not necessary* or in some other way failed to contribute to the poem as a whole. He would cut and cut again, but seldom add, other than to replace a word or phrase with a better word or phrase.

Study of the manuscripts confirmed my hunch about Yeats's habits of composition. He did tend to move from the subjective to the objective as, for example, in the little poem 'Memory', a draft of which reads:

> One had a lovely face
> And two or three had charm
> But face & charm were in vain
> I could not change for the grass
> Cannot but keep the form
> Where the mountain hare has lain[.]

In revision, line 4 became 'Because the mountain grass'. The 'I' is similarly edited out of the opening stanza of a number of poems (including 'Sailing to Byzantium' and 'Byzantium'). The

'I' of the drafts becomes 'we' in others (such as 'After Long Silence' and 'The Black Tower'), as if by admitting other people – even, perhaps, his reader – to share a poem's stage with him, Yeats sought to give it more of the authority of universality. But the most striking reduction of the subjective element occurs in 'A Prayer for my Daughter', at the end of which three stanzas about himself are replaced by one about his daughter, the principal subject of the poem.

★

By the middle of August I was running out of money and, more importantly, knew I had enough material for the thesis I was now admitting to myself I wanted to write. When, on my last afternoon, I brought back from the Library W.B.'s notebooks and manuscripts, Mrs Yeats said 'Let's celebrate! Ring the Shelbourne Hotel and book a table in my name.'

I was touched but at the same time (it hurts me to confess) horrified. My clothes were unsuitable for Dublin's grandest hotel, as were such as I had seen of Mrs Yeats's.

'How about something a little less . . . majestic?'

'No,' she said, 'this is an occasion for the Shelbourne,' and so to the Shelbourne we went – she in her felt hat, me in my out-at-elbows jacket. As I followed her sheepishly through the revolving door, a minor miracle occurred. The braying Ascendancy crowd in the foyer divided and fell silent, as the hotel's frock-coated Manager swept forward to welcome her and escort us to 'Your usual table, Mrs Yeats'. It was the best in the chandeliered dining-room and, as our napkins were shaken out for us, the Chef appeared to present his menu to the Honoured Guest. 'Only in Ireland,' I thought to myself, remembering the question and answer ending Yeats's play, *Cathleen Ni Houlihan*:

'Did you see an old woman going down the path?
'I did not, but I saw a young girl, and she had the walk of a queen.'

My Fairy Godmother was in magical form, regaling me – and everyone within earshot – with stories from a lifetime as an Archpoet's consort and muse and, since 1939, keeper of the shrine. She was alarmingly well-read, in French and Italian as well as English, and disarmingly funny – paticularly about self-proclaimed poets and supposed scholars. It was then she told me that, at our first meeting, she had given me the most difficult notebooks 'as a test. I have to find out', she explained, 'if someone's a *real* poetry person, or play person, or prose person.'

'But I could have told you I was a poetry person,' I said.

'It's not what *you* think you are,' she replied, 'it's what *I* think you are!' I asked if some people failed her test.

'Indeed!' she said.

★

Before going to the airport next morning, I stopped to say goodbye and give her some roses. She waved me on my way with an unexpected word of advice:

'So long, and don't spend all your life on Yeats.'

'I won't,' I said and, even as I said it, I knew that the poem in my pocket was more important to me than all the transcriptions in my suitcase – and tomorrow's poem was more important still.

8

Afterword

WHY SHOULD THE parent of one or two legitimate poems make
a public display of the illegitimate offspring of his apprentice
years? The short answer is because, to the best of my knowledge,
no one else has done so, and the schooling of poets seems a potentially rewarding subject. In the early chapters of their autobiographies, Coleridge, Hardy, Yeats, Sassoon, Graves, Day
Lewis, Spender, and MacNeice have a good deal to say about the
external circumstances of their family lives, but little about their
internal or 'writerly' lives. MacNeice, in a critical book *Modern
Poetry*, does offer case studies of his own reading and (to a lesser
extent, writing) in childhood, at public school, and at Oxford. It
was while trying to develop those impressionistic sketches into a
comprehensive account of his poetic apprenticeship that I began
to reflect on this curious omission in the autobiographies of
poets; an omission no biographer can properly rectify. This
reflection led this biographer to conduct an experiment he will
count at least a partial success if it encourages better poets to write
better accounts of their apprenticeship. But even if it achieves
nothing else, it has shown me things about biography I didn't
know, and led me to question some of its current conventions.

First, it has led me at certain points to ask what I – as a
biographer, with no privileged knowledge of my subject –
would have made of the evidence available to me. All too often,

the answer is I should have reached the wrong conclusion or overlooked a crucial conjunction. This attempt at a self-portrait of the would-be artist is based on a fraction of the research underlying my portraits of Owen and MacNeice, but I've no doubt it is truer to the life of its subject.

Those earlier biographies followed the convention that proscribes the use of direct speech other than in quotation from a contemporary source. This now seems to me illogical. Since there can be no guarantee of the accuracy of *any* speech not mechanically recorded, it is possible – if not probable – that all recorded speech transcribed from memory is to some extent inaccurate. Should no such records then be admitted in historical or auto/biographical writing? I can remember, at least in outline and often in some detail, conversations that were important to me. Must all reference to these be omitted because, in a court of law, I couldn't swear to their complete accuracy? I have given myself the benefit of the doubt, on the grounds that, provided a caveat is offered as to the use of imaginative cement in reassembling the shards of conversation, a reconstruction is better than nothing. Such a caveat is offered here.

The autobiographer has many advantages over the biographer: not only a closer relationship with his subject, but a better sense of the material *not* available to him, and its importance. If no evidence remains of an influence, a friendship, a love affair, he can at least attempt to reconstruct it; and he may grant himself a licence (denied the conscientious biographer) to omit whatever he thinks boring or irrelevant to his design. In other words, the proportions of an autobiography – unlike those of a biography – need not be determined by the proportional spread of available evidence.

*

I'm grateful to a number of people who assisted my experiment with help of one kind or another: Sarah Barker, Betty Barrett,

Hugo Brunner, Sandie Byrne, Barry Cunningham-Batt, Mary D'Arcy, Robin Davies, Ruth Escritt, Peter France, Laurel Glockner, Colin Harris, Michael Harrison, Robin Houghton, Jenny Houlsby, Mary Jacobus, Kenneth and Wendy Jennings, Anne and Richard Keynes, Stephen Keynes, Tony Kirk-Greene, Barbara Lynam, Grant McIntyre, Rusty MacLean, Jackie Scott-Mandeville, John Marshall, Michael Metcalf, Bernard and Heather O'Donoghue, Ros Patten, John Penney, Gail Pirkis, Judith Priestman, John and Jay Rendall, Richard and Kate Sorabji, and Jim and Sally Thompson.

My greatest debt, however, is to my wife Jill and children Pippa and Nick, for reading and questioning these memoirs of an incomplete stranger.

Notes

The sources of information and quotation in the text are identified below by the number of the page on which they appear. Quotations are identified by the first words quoted.

Chapter 1: Genealogy

p. 10 'the ghost of some': T.S. Eliot, 'Reflections on *Vers Libre*' in *To Criticize the Critics*, Faber, 1965, p. 187.

p. 13 'A Letter from Berlin': Jon Stallworthy, *Root and Branch*, Chatto & Windus, 1969, pp. 55–6.

p. 15 'Swift of foot': 'The Song of Hiawatha' in H.W. Longfellow, *Poetical Works*, Oxford University Press, 1904, p. 213.

p. 16 'Peter gave himself': Beatrix Potter, *The Tale of Peter Rabbit*, Frederick Warne, n.d., p. 33.

p. 17 'The King's Breakfast' and 'Bad Sir Brian Botany': A.A. Milne, *When We Were Very Young*, Methuen, 1924, pp. 55 and 92.

p. 19 'The Old Sailor': A.A. Milne, *Now We Are Six*, Methuen, 1927, p. 36.

Chapter 2: Mythology and History

p. 24 'The Oxford Preparatory School': for the history of the Dragon School, see C.H. Jaques, *A Dragon Centenary 1877–1977*, privately printed, 1977 (hereafter *Jaques*).

p. 24 'It must have been': *Jaques*, p. 2.

p. 27 'On the morning': *Jaques*, p. 141.

p. 32 'Miss Lavender': Jon Stallworthy, *Out of Bounds*, Oxford University Press, 1963, p. 2.

Chapter 3: Latin

p. 36 'Onward Christian Soldiers': by S. Baring-Gould, see *Hymns Ancient and Modern Revised*, Hymns Ancient and Modern, 1916 (hereafter *Hymns A & M*), p. 867.

p. 39 'the British had chosen': James Morris, *Farewell the Trumpets: An Imperial Retreat*, Faber, 1978, p. 21.

p. 40 'We are the happy legion': 'Absolution' in *The War Poems of Siegfried Sassoon*, ed. Rupert Hart-Davis, Faber, 1983, p. 15.

p. 40 'The battle was long': Caesar, *The Gallic War*, trans. H.J. Edwards, William Heinemann Ltd and Harvard University Press, 1917, pp. 167–8.

p. 45 'O valiant hearts': John S. Arkwright, 'For the Fallen', *Hymns A & M*, p. 791.

p. 45 'They shall grow': Laurence Binyon, 'For the Fallen', see *The New Oxford Book of English Verse*, ed. Helen Gardner, Clarendon Press, 1972 (hereafter *Gardner*), pp. 831–2.

p. 45 'Do not despair': 'For Johnny' in John Pudney, *Dispersal Point*, John Lane, The Bodley Head, 1942, p. 24.

p. 46 'There are Dragons': *Jaques*, pp. 30–2.

p. 60 'Memorableness is one': S.P.B. Mais, *The Draconian*, Christmas 1945, p. 10538.

p. 61 'Friend of my youth': John Betjeman, *New Bats in Old Belfries*, John Murray, 1945 (hereafter *Betjeman*), p. 53.

p. 62 'Miss J. Hunter Dunn': 'A Subaltern's Love Song' in *Betjeman*, p. 5.

p. 62 'she walked unaware': 'She Walked Unaware' by Thomas MacDonagh, see *The Oxford Book of Irish Verse*, ed. Donagh MacDonagh and Lennox Robinson, Oxford University Press, 1958, p. 248.

p. 65 'Time, like an ever-rolling': Isaac Watts, 'O God our help in ages past', see *Hymns A & M*, p. 217.

Notes

p. 66 'Where the bee sucks': William Shakespeare, *The Tempest*, V.i. 88–9.

p. 67 'In one slight pause': F.E.H.[icks], 'The River', *The Draconian*, Summer 1948, p. 11019.

Chapter 4: Metrics

p. 68 'Cheerful, and helpful': 'Rugby Chapel' in *The Poems of Matthew Arnold*, ed. Kenneth Allott, Longman, 1965 (hereafter *Arnold*), p. 452.

p. 68 'a magnificent Roman camp': Thomas Hughes, *Tom Brown's Schooldays*, Macmillan paperback, 1958 (hereafter *Brown*), p. 18.

p. 69 'From the cradle': *Brown*, pp. 242–3.

p. 70 'The field/Strewn': 'Rugby Chapel' in *Arnold*, pp. 444–5.

p. 71 'If I should die': 'The Soldier' in *Rupert Brooke: The Poetical Works*, ed. Geoffrey Keynes, Faber, 1946 (hereafter *Brooke*), p. 23.

p. 72 'Greenstreet's Prince Hal': *The Draconian*, Summer 1945, p. 10460.

p. 80 'My dear Triumvir': quoted in Geoffrey Keynes, *The Gates of Memory*, Oxford University Press, 1981 (hereafter *Keynes*), pp. 67–8.

p. 83 'That summer': *Keynes*, pp. 150–2.

p. 84 'Here of a Sunday': 'Bredon Hill' in *The Collected Poems of A.E. Housman*, Jonathan Cape, 1939, p. 35.

p. 85 'She was working': Margaret Elizabeth Keynes, *A House by the River: Newnham Grange to Darwin College*, Darwin College, Cambridge, 1976, pp. 196–203.

p. 92 'Andrew Marvell's poem': see *Gardner*, p. 336.

p. 94 'On First Looking': 'That it was Balboa, not Cortez who caught his first sight of the Pacific from the heights of Darien, in Panama, matters to history but not to poetry': *The Norton Anthology of English Literature*, ed. M.H. Abrams *et al.*, W.W. Norton, 6th ed., 1993, vol. 2, p. 769.

p. 95 'CAMARET EN FÊTE': *The New Rugbeian*, V, 6, December 1951, p. 186.

p. 98 'The round earth's': John Donne, 'Holy Sonnets' 7, see *Gardner*, p. 197.

Chapter 5: Dinnschenchas

p. 99 'Dirty British coaster': John Masefield, 'Cargoes', see *Gardner*, p. 845.

p. 99 'Nobly, nobly': Robert Browning, 'Home-Thoughts from the Sea', see *Gardner*, p. 661.

p. 102 'My garage': Ursula Bethell, 'Detail' in *An Anthology of New Zealand Verse*, selected by Robert Chapman and Jonathan Bennett, Oxford University Press, 1956 (hereafter *Chapman and Bennett*), p. 80.

p. 103 'It would not be': Ursula Bethell, 'The Long Harbour' in *Chapman and Bennett*, p. 82.

p. 103 'Often in summer': James K. Baxter, 'Wild Bees' in *Chapman and Bennett*, pp. 243–4.

p. 106 'In peaceful times': 'Rugby' in *The Draconian*, Easter 1953, p. 11940.

p. 107 'adopting his title': 'Rugby Chapel', *The New Rugbeian*, V, 9, June 1953, p. 282.

p. 110 'Every man thinks': G.B. Hill and L.F. Powell, eds., *Boswell's Life of Johnson*, Clarendon Press, 1934, vol. 3, p. 265.

p. 110 'Perpetua': *The New Rugbeian*, Coronation Number, V, 9, June 1953, p. 264.

p. 116 'And I was filled': Siegfried Sassoon, 'Everyone Sang', see *Gardner*, p. 862.

p. 121 'For the fors': quoted in Ian Brinkworth, *One-Eyed Man is King*, Cassell, 1996, p. 320.

p. 123 'we feel the far track': 'Bridge-Guard in the Karroo' in *The Definitive Edition of Rudyard Kipling's Verse*, Hodder and Stoughton, 1940, pp. 205–7.

p. 124 'We buried him': Charles Wolfe, 'The Burial of Sir John Moore after Corunna', see *Gardner*, pp. 579–80.

p. 128 'happy Warrior': 'Character of the Happy Warrior' in William Wordsworth, *Poems*, ed. John O. Hayden, vol. I, Penguin Books, 1977, p. 662.

p. 134 'tired the sun': William Cory, 'Heraclitus', see *Gardner*, p. 705.

p. 140 'Into her dream': 'The Eve of St Agnes' in *The Poems of John Keats*, ed. Miriam Allott, Longman, 1970, p. 475.

p. 144 'Busy old fool': John Donne, 'The Sun Rising', see *Gardner*, p. 191.

Chapter 6: Public Performance

p. 149 '*Sweets to the sweet*': William Shakespeare, *Hamlet*, V.i. 244.

p. 151 '*Byrhtwold mathelode*': 'The Battle of Maldon' in *Sweet's Anglo-Saxon Reader in Prose and Verse*, rev. C.T. Onions, Clarendon Press, 1954, p. 120.

p. 151 'soaked in blood': Aneirin, 'The Gododdin', *The Earliest Welsh Poems*, trans. Joseph P. Clancy, Macmillan, 1970.

p. 153 'Where those consumed': *The Eclogues, Georgics and Aeneid of Virgil*, trans. C. Day Lewis, Oxford University Press, 1966, pp. 298–9.

p. 158 'a tale I have heard': 'Waikiki' in *Brooke*, p. 37.

p. 163 'count those feathered': 'Meditations in Time of Civil War', V, in *Collected Poems of W.B. Yeats*, Macmillan, 1950, p. 230.

p. 164 'And the first grey': 'Sohrab and Rustum' in *Arnold*, p. 304.

p. 164 'Soon a hum': 'Sohrab and Rustum' in *Arnold*, p. 330.

p. 164 'At home': 'Oxford' in *The Complete Poems of Keith Douglas*, ed. Desmond Graham, Oxford University Press, 1978, p. 68.

p. 167 'Now as I was young': 'Fern Hill' in *Dylan Thomas: Collected Poems, 1934–1952*, J.M. Dent & Sons, 1952, p. 159.

p. 167 'Already the bull': 'Lament for the Death of a Bullfighter' in Federico García Lorca, *Lament for the Death of a Bullfighter and Other Poems*, trans. A.L. Lloyd, Heinemann, 1953, pp. 34–5.

p. 169 'Oxford owed': 'Oxford's Good Victory', *Manchester Guardian*, 10 October 1956, p. 8.

p. 169 'Neither of the four': 'No Reputations Made in Trials', *Oxford Mail*, 16 October 1956, p. 7.

p. 171 'The forwards responded': 'Oxford Greyhounds' Good Win', *Manchester Guardian*, 31 October 1956, p. 9.

p. 172 'it cannot be hidden': 'Greyhounds Defeat Oxford', *The Times*, 31 October 1956, p. 12.

p. 180 'The gross sun': 'Song' in Dom Moraes, *A Beginning*, The Parton Press, 1957, p. 10 (hereafter *Moraes*).

p. 180 'Moz': *Moraes*, p. 13.

p. 182 'Then wilt thou': *Paradise Lost* in *The Poems of John Milton*, ed. John Carey and Alastair Fowler, Longmans, 1968 (hereafter *Milton*), Book XII, lines 585–7.

p. 191 'spoken by one': Anon., *Oratio Creweiana/MCMLVIII*, printed at the University Press, Oxford, 1958, p. 21; the Latin is given on p. 20.

p. 194 'I think a railroad': *The Letters of W.B. Yeats*, ed. Allan Wade, Rupert Hart-Davis, 1954, p. 427.

p. 194 'Here and There': Jon Stallworthy, *The Astronomy of Love*, Oxford University Press, 1961 (hereafter *Astronomy*), p. 13.

p. 196 'He hadde a thombe': 'General Prologue' to *The Canterbury Tales* in *The Works of Geoffrey Chaucer*, ed. F.N. Robinson, Oxford University Press, 2nd ed., 1988, p. 22.

p. 198 'The isles of Greece': Lord Byron, 'The Isles of Greece', see *Gardner*, p. 575.

Chapter 7: Irish Manuscripts

p. 203 'To Maurice Bowra': W.B. Yeats, quoted in C.M. Bowra, *Memories: 1898–1939*, Weidenfeld and Nicolson, 1966, p. 242.

p. 203 'Homer had not sung': 'Meditations in Time of Civil War', I, in *Collected Poems of W.B. Yeats*, Macmillan, 1950 (hereafter *Yeats*), p. 225.

p. 204 'The mad wind': Maurice Bowra, *The Heritage of Symbolism*, Macmillan, 1943, p. 172.

p. 206 'The Twelve': Alexander Blok, *The Twelve and Other Poems*, trans. Jon Stallworthy and Peter France, Eyre & Spottiswoode, 1970, pp. 141–60.

p. 206 '*A Familiar Tree*': Jon Stallworthy, *A Familiar Tree*, Chatto & Windus and Oxford University Press, 1978.

p. 206 'with Peter France': *Boris Pasternak: Selected Poems*, trans. Jon Stallworthy and Peter France, Allen Lane, 1983.

p. 207 'Lombard's forwards': 'Little to Acclaim at Oxford', *The Times*, 10 October 1958, p. 18.

p. 207 'In hooking': 'One-sided Oxford Final Trial', *The Times*, 17 October 1958, p. 19.

p. 207 'like greyhounds': William Shakespeare, *Henry V*, III.i. 31–2.

p. 207 '[The University] scraped': 'Oxford Win Poor Match', *Manchester Guardian*, 6 November 1958, p. 4.

p. 208 'It took': 'Greyhounds Show the Way', *Manchester Guardian*, 5 December 1958, p. 6.

p. 210 'Like an hysterical': 'Edmund Spenser' in W.B. Yeats, *Essays and Introductions*, Macmillan, 1961, pp. 361 and 372–4.

p. 211 'The Curse of Cromwell': *Yeats*, p. 350.

p. 212 'Walking – but you': 'Where are the Songs of Spring?' *Astronomy*, p. 19.

p. 213 'a terrible mistake': 'Oxford Puntsmen lose poles – and the race', *Manchester Guardian*, 15 June 1959, p. 3.

p. 213 'All Rome sent': 'Horatius' in *The Works of Lord Macaulay*, vol. II, Longmans Green, 1898, p. 359.

p. 213 'Camus, reverend sire': 'Lycidas' in *Milton*, p. 247, line 103.

p. 217 'Crookedly broken nose': Robert Graves, 'The Face in the Mirror' in *New Collected Poems*, Doubleday & Company, 1977, p. 139.

p. 219 'Lapis Lazuli': *Yeats*, p. 375.

p. 224 'Yeats's "Statues"': *Yeats*, p. 375.

p. 224 '*monumentum aere*' [Latin for 'the memorial more enduring than brass']: Horace, *Odes*, III.xxx.1.

p. 224 'The Municipal Gallery': *Yeats*, p. 368.

p. 225 'Still Life': *Astronomy*, p. 48.

p. 227 'Memory': This draft appears in Jon Stallworthy, *Between the Lines:Yeats's Poetry in the Making*, Clarendon Press, 1963, p. 205. The drafts of 'Sailing to Byzantium' and 'Byzantium', 'After Long Silence', 'The Black Tower', and 'A Prayer for my Daughter' are discussed, respectively, on pp. 87–136, 209–10, 222–42, and 26–45.

p. 228 '*Cathleen Ni Houlihan*': *The Collected Plays of W.B. Yeats*, Macmillan, 2nd ed., 1952, p. 88.

Chapter 8: Afterword

p. 230 '*Modern Poetry*': Louis MacNeice, *Modern Poetry: A Personal Essay*, Oxford University Press, 1938, pp. 31–74.

Acknowledgements

The author and publisher wish to thank the following for permission to reproduce extracts from copyright material:

The Caxton Press: Ursula Bethell, 'Detail' and 'The Long Harbour' in *An Anthology of New Zealand Verse*, selected by Robert Chapman and Jonathan Bennett, Oxford University Press, 1956; The Dragon School Trust Ltd: C.H. Jaques, *A Dragon Centenary, 1877–1977*, privately printed, 1977; David Higham Associates: John Pudney, 'For Johnny' in *Dispersal Point*, John Lane, The Bodley Head, 1942; John Murray (Publishers) Ltd: John Betjeman, 'In Memory of Basil, Marquess of Dufferin and Ava' and 'A Subaltern's Love-Song' in *New Bats in Old Belfries*, John Murray, 1945; Oxford University Press: James K. Baxter, 'Wild Bees' in *An Anthology of New Zealand Verse*, selected by Robert Chapman and Jonathan Bennett, Oxford University Press, 1956; and A.P. Watt Ltd. on behalf of Michael Yeats: 'Meditations in Time of Civil War', 'The Curse of Cromwell', 'Lapis Lazuli', 'The Statues', 'The Municipal Gallery Revisited', and 'Memory' in *Collected Poems of W.B. Yeats*, Macmillan, 1950; 'To Maurice Bowra' in C.M. Bowra, *Memories: 1898–1939*, Weidenfeld and Nicolson, 1966; *The Letters of W.B. Yeats*, ed. Allan Wade, Rupert Hart-Davis, 1954; 'Edmund Spenser' in W.B. Yeats, *Essays and Introductions*, Macmillan, 1961; *Cathleen Ni Houlihan* in *The Collected Plays of W.B. Yeats*, Macmillan, 2nd ed., 1952; dedication to *Reveries over Childhood and Youth*, Macmillan, 1926.

Index

Index

Hardy, Thomas: autobiography (*The Life of Thomas Hardy: 1840–1928*; ostensibly by Florence E. Hardy, but all except last few years by TH himself), 230

Hare, John, 118, 124–7, 133

Hayward, Max, 205–6

'Here and There' (JS; poem), 194–5

H[icks], F.E.: 'The River', 67

'High Tide' (JS; poem), 141–2

Hoare, Jack, 171–2, 181–2

Hoffmann, Heinrich: 'Story of Johnny-Head-in-Air', 46

Hopkins, Gerard Manley, 150, 184

Horace: *Odes*, 223

Housman, A.E.: 'Bredon Hill', 84

Howie family, 2–3, *3*, 12

Howie, John (JS's maternal grandfather), 2–3

Howie, John Ruskin (JS's uncle), 2, 98, 100

Howie, Margaret (*née* Todd; JS's maternal grandmother), 2–3, 5

Howie, Tennyson (JS's uncle), 2–3, 5

Howie, William Gladstone (JS's uncle), 2–4, 100

Hughes, Thomas: *Tom Brown's Schooldays*, 68–9, 73

Ibadan University, 133

Ireland (Magdalen College scout), 178

Jacqueline (French friend), 95, 168

Jalengo (Nigerian soldier), 132

James, Henry, 80–1

Jaques, C.H.: *A Dragon Centenary 1877–1977*, 24, 27, 46

Jean (Lammas House cook), 82–3, 90

Jemima (London landlady), 8, 12

Jesson, D., 206

Johnson, Lionel: 'By the Statue of King Charles at Charing Cross', 44

Jones, Emrys, 149

Jones, Nancy, 5

Julian (army friend), 113–15, 117–18

Kadilla (polo pony), 125–8, *126*, 138, 145

Keats, John: as 'dresser' at Bart's Hospital, 8; early death, 81; on writing long poems, 174; 'La Belle Dame Sans Merci', 44, 78–9; 'The Eve of St Agnes', 140, 154; 'On First Looking into Chapman's Homer', 94

Ketton-Kremer, Wyndham, 214–16

Keyes, Sidney, 159

Keynes, Sir Geoffrey: at Bart's Hospital, 8; visits Rugby School, 79–82; JS visits at Lammas House, Brinkley, 82–92; courtship and marriage, 83–5; portrait, *88*; craftsmanship and practicality, 89–91; book collecting and bibliography, 90–1; croquet, 93; gives Yeats bibliography to JS, 208; camping at Felbrigg with JS, 214–16; *The Gates of Memory*, 80, 84

Keynes, Margaret Elizabeth, Lady (*née* Darwin): courtship and marriage, 83–5; at Lammas House, 83, 86–7, 93; works in Naval Intelligence, 84–5; gardening, 92; *A House by the River*, 85

Kipling, Rudyard, 46–7; 'Bridge-Guard in the Karroo', 123; *Puck of Pook's Hill*, 46; 'Song to Mithras', 47

Lagos, Nigeria, 134–5, 138, 145

Lammas House, Brinkley (Suffolk), 82–90, *86*

Landor, Walter Savage, 70

Lavender, Miss (riding instructress), 32

Lawrence, D.H.: *Sons and Lovers*, 134

'Letter from Berlin, A' (JS; poem), 13–14

'Leviathan' (JS; poem), 174–6, 178

Lewis, Clive Staples, 149

Liddell, Henry George, Dean of Christ Church, Oxford, 24

Liddell, Lionel Charles, 24

Lloyd, A.L., 167

Lloyd-Jones, David, 159

Lombard, Theo, 206–7

Longfellow, Henry Wadsworth: 'The Song of Hiawatha', 15

Lopdell, Merlyn (JS's cousin), 102, 111

Lorca, Federico García: 'Lament for the Death of a Bullfighter', 167–8

Lynam, C.C. ('the Skipper'), 23, 25–7, *26*, 44, 50

Lynam, A.E. ('Hum'), 30, 36, 45, 65–6, *66*

Lynam, Joc, 30, 36, 53–5, *54*, 63

Macaulay, Thomas Babington, Baron, 39, 46; 'Horatius', 213

MacDonagh, Thomas: 'She Walked Unaware', 62

'Machine Gun, The' (JS; poem), 82

McLean, Dennis, 170

MacLochlainn, Alf, 221

Index

Index

Rugby School: JS prepares for, 63, 68; JS attends, 69–74, 106; poetry prize, 92–5; school dance, 112–13

Sassoon, Siegfried: autobiography (*The Complete Memoirs of George Sherston*), 230; 'Absolution', 40; 'Everyone Sang', 116
'School Dance' (JS; poem), 112–13
Seekers, The (film), 117
Seferis, George, 206
Selig, Richard: at Oxford, 159; death and obituary, 179, 181
Shakespeare, William, 64; *Hamlet*, 149; *Henry V*, 207; *The Tempest*, 44, 66
Shotover Edge (house): Stallworthy family moves to, 56–8, 57
Skipper, the *see* Lynam, C.C.
Solomons, Bethel, 216–18
'Somewhere between February and March 1955' (JS; poem), 135–7
Sorabji, Kate (*née* Taster): courtship and marriage, 177–8, 210
Sorabji, Richard Rustom Kharsedji: at Dragon School, 48–50, 48; JS's friendship with, 60; military service, 110; music and singing at Oxford, 159, 177, 187; holds Oxford May Day party with JS, 163–4; cheated by pub landlord, 187; marriage, 210
Sorley, Charles Hamilton, 43
South Africa: JS's parents visit, 176
Spain: JS holidays in, 165–8
Spender, Sir Stephen: on Dom Moraes, 180; autobiography (*World Within World*), 230
Spenser, Edmund: Yeats on, 208; on Irish poets, 218; *The Faerie Queene*, 44, 109, 154; *View of the Present State of Ireland*, 209
Stallworthy family, 4
Stallworthy, John Arthur (JS's father): in New Zealand, 3–5, 58; engagement and marriage, 5, 7; medical career, 5, 8, 12–13, 34; moves to England, 7–8; early financial difficulties, 8–9; motoring, 12, 33; studies in Germany, 13; portrait, 22; in sailing accident, 28–9; teaches rugby to JS, 31–2; wartime emergency service, 33, 35; acquires Shotover Edge, 56–8; watches JS's rugby-playing, 58, 63, 169–70, 181; and JS at Rugby, 69–70; tree-planting, 69; Visiting

Professorship in Sydney, 97, 101; and Jack Bennett, 149–50; operates in South Africa, 176–7; celebrates JS's return from Greece, 199–200
Stallworthy, Peggy (Margaret; *née* Howie; JS's mother): family background, 2–3, 5; engagement and marriage, 5, 7; moves to England, 7–8; singing, 9–10; recites and reads to JS, 10–12, 16, 27; portrait, 22; intervenes in street fracas, 28; birth of twin daughters, 35; advises on JS's prize poem, 94; leaves for Australia, 97–100; revisits New Zealand (1952), 101–2, 104; lends car to JS for Spanish holiday, 165; visit to South Africa, 176; celebrates JS's return from Greece, 199
Stallworthy, Sally and Wendy (JS's twin sisters): born, 35; 98
Stevens, Tom, 188–9
'Still Life' (JS; poem), 225
Sweet's Anglo-Saxon Primer, 148–50
Swift, Jonathan: *A Modest Proposal*, 76 & n
Sydney, Australia, 97, 101

Taster, Kate *see* Sorabji, Kate
Templeton (New Zealand lawyer), 6–7
Tennyson, Alfred, 1st Baron: 'The Lady of Shalott', 44; 'Morte d'Arthur', 44; 'The Revenge', 44
Thomas, Dylan, 167–8, 174–5, 225; 'Fern Hill', 167
Times, The, 172, 207
Tosswill, T.D.: teaches JS at Rugby, 76, 78; portrait, 77; introduces JS to Keynes, 79–82; runs school English Club, 79, 119; comments on JS's Newdigate poems, 158, 174–5, 187; recommends Yeats to JS, 158, 163
Trinity College, Dublin, 216, 220–1

Umoru Lai (Nigerian sergeant), 120
United States of America: JS visits, 176
Usika Dila (Nigerian soldier), 132

VE Day (8 May 1945), 57
Virgil: *Aeneid*, 151–4

Wade, Allan: *Bibliography of the Writings of W.B. Yeats*, 208
Waikiwi, New Zealand, 2–3

245